FREEDOM FROM FEAR

Also by the same author:

Wing Chun Kung Fu: An Effective and Logical Approach to Self-Defence, Karen Armstrong and Sifu Jim Fung (1980, 1981, rev. 1986)

The Authentic Wing Chun Weapons: Long Pole and Butterfly Knives, Master Jim Fung and Karen Armstrong (1986)

Distributed by Bookwise International, Findon SA (08) 268 8222

FREEDOM FROM FEAR

A complete guide to personal safety for women

KAREN ARMSTRONG

ALLEN & UNWIN

DEDICATION

To my beloved mother Joan—
thank you for the gift of life and love

First published 1994
Allen & Unwin Pty Ltd
9 Atchison Street, St Leonards, NSW 2065 Australia

National Library of Australia
Cataloguing–in–Publication entry

Armstrong, Karen (Karen Rosemary).
  Freedom from fear: a complete guide to personal
  safety for women.

  Includes index.
  ISBN 1 86373 658 1.

  1. Self-defence for women. 1. Title.

613.66

Designed by Christie & Eckermann
Printed by Alken Press, NSW
10 9 8 7 6 5 4 3 2 1

CONTENTS

ACKNOWLEDGMENTS

A big thank you to the many people who have assisted me with this book. Important information and contacts were provided by Claire Vernon and Eileen Graham at the NSW Health Department, Robert Jochelson and Roseanne Bonney at the NSW Bureau of Crime Statistics and Research, Jane Bridge and Vanessa O'Mara at the NSW Office for the Status of Women, Sergeant Kim McKay from the Community Safety Development Branch of the NSW Police Service, and John Walker and Ingrid Wilson at the Institute of Criminology. Andrew Farthing has done an excellent job with the photographs; my 'attackers', Dave Shelley, Paul Lampis, Greg Buxton, Beau Bouzaid and Boris Osidacz performed their task with enthusiasm. Helen Burnie gave valuable advice on the text.

Wing Chun experts Jim Fung, Tsui Seung Tin and Graham Kuerschner taught me this fabulous martial art. John Haralambides at Odyssey Clothing offered wardrobe assistance. My husband Colin and daughter Shannon gave me love and support. Lynne Frolich at Allen & Unwin was a true professional. My appreciation extends to the wider circle of friends and colleagues who have taken an interest in this project, and to everyone who is working towards reducing violence.

Feedback and enquiries are invited from readers, and can be addressed to me through Allen & Unwin.

Introduction

I am concerned about violence, especially violence towards those who are most vulnerable—women, children and older people. I don't like the idea of being attacked so I have taken steps to face this fear and to deal with it constructively. This process has transformed my whole life and given me skills of personal protection that I would like to share with women all over Australia.

I have distilled the essence of my knowledge into *Freedom From Fear*. This is a 'can do' book rather than a heavy training manual. It contains vital information and the techniques that women need for total safety. You don't need to be a martial arts exponent—these methods can be used by anyone.

I used to believe that because women are usually smaller than men we wouldn't have much chance of getting away if attacked. Now I know this is not true. I have discovered an inner power that enables me to remain calm under pressure, to be more assertive in everyday situations and to face potential attack situations with increased courage and determination.

My desire for self-empowerment was aroused years ago as a teenager. I was walking with a girlfriend through deserted university grounds one evening when we were approached by four young men. I was getting ready to talk them out of any evil intentions they may have had, but to my enormous surprise my girlfriend quickly pounced into a martial arts fighting stance and gave a loud shout that pierced the cool night. The men were even more surprised than I, and visibly moved backwards; within seconds they had melted into the darkness. That sold me—I had never seen or heard anything like this before!

For eighteen years I trained in various forms of martial arts, mainly Wing Chun Kung Fu—the only system founded by a woman and tailor-made for women's physical capacities. The movements are incredibly simple and effective. I felt as if I'd discovered the eighth wonder of the world.

Since then I have taught safety awareness to thousands of people from all walks of life and seen them transform in confidence, fitness, self-esteem and freedom from fear. I have also learnt that self defence is only one part of being safe. Many dangerous situations can be avoided and defused before there is any need for self-defence skills. But I noticed that women who had these skills were much more aware and therefore able to avoid danger; they were also more confident and therefore able to use other strategies, knowing that in the last resort they could fight back. Inner confidence is the ultimate survival strategy.

Every woman can discover both the psychological and physical skills that will give her increased control, confidence and safety in her life. *Freedom From Fear* outlines a simple, complete approach to personal protection. This book will reveal and enhance the survival skills you already possess. You will learn a wide repertoire of responses that empower you to deal with situations from the most minor to a life-threatening attack. Because no two women or situations are the same, a variety of responses are presented, enabling you to choose those you feel most comfortable with.

Commonsense concepts will enable you to prevent and avoid danger. You can learn to recognise and avert risk situations, to defuse potentially dangerous events and to fight back effectively when necessary. In Chapters 3, 4 and 5, we will examine the options available; you may be pleasantly surprised to find that there are more effective choices than you were previously aware of. A strong emphasis is placed on prevention, avoidance and defusing, so that fighting back is usually a last resort. In some situations it is the only choice.

Chapters 4 and 5 on fighting back show you how to use your body with amazing efficiency, helping you to develop and project confidence to an attacker and telling him you are not a victim. This deters many would-be attackers.

While there is no guarantee of total safety, I can promise that your chances of being *safer* in every situation will be greatly improved by absorbing the knowledge in this book. It is like a map to help you in your own process of facing fear and discovering personal power.

Amidst all the negative messages women receive about the dangers of being attacked, this book has a message of optimism and personal power. Women can avoid, defuse, defend and win! We have the right to be free from the fear of intimidation and attack.

Chapter 1

'COULD IT HAPPEN TO ME?'

I was less than a block away from home that evening when a car with five young men drove up beside me. Two of them jumped out, grabbed me and pulled me into the backseat . . . I felt very frightened at first. I have always been a passive person, taught to compromise instead of use force . . . But as I sat there, I began to get angry. I sat quietly while we rode to an old cemetery. When they stopped the car, I was ready . . . I bit the arm that held me, hit the guy behind me in the gut with my right elbow and kicked the guy coming toward me, all at the same time. The one holding me let go, and the one facing me got out of the car, hurt. I got out of the car quickly and ran. The other men were so surprised, they didn't move fast enough to stop me. (Groves & Caignon: 1989, p. 182)

What is of value in your life? Sometimes we take the most valuable things for granted. We insure our cars, our houses and other property, but what do we do about our personal safety? This asset, which cannot be replaced, deserves our utmost protection. Despite all the social changes that have taken place in women's lives, we still cannot go about our everyday activities without the subtle reminder we could be attacked. Day and night, women everywhere are aware, through a kind of sixth sense, of the possibility of violence.

One of the first steps for a woman to overcome the fear of being attacked is to say: 'It could happen to me. What would I do? Would I run, shout, fight? Would fear restrict my responses?'

Once we face the possibility of attack, we open up a whole

range of options that we can use to protect our safety. As each woman discovers the responses that are most natural for her she is able to increase her inner strength and confidence.

Prevention is the best approach for women who want to fully enjoy their lives. After an attack, life is never quite the same again. Your former carefree confidence, your ability to be spontaneous, your openness to take on new challenges, may change.

Protecting your safety means placing a high value on your body and your peace of mind, for these are the assets usually violated by an attack. It means investing some of your resources—time, energy, money—into preventing, preparing, protecting. It means making safety awareness a positive part of your daily life.

VIOLENCE TO WOMEN

Violence is an unavoidable aspect of life. We hear and read about assaults, robberies, sexual assaults, abductions and murders. While these are not cheerful topics, they are certainly prevalent, as any casual scan of a newspaper will show. Most people know someone, either directly or indirectly, who has been attacked. There is often a sense of shame attached to being the victim of an attack, particularly of sexual assault or domestic violence. This makes it hard for many people to share their experiences openly. It also keeps the true dimensions of the problem hidden.

For many women, an underlying sense of fear and vulnerability may come to the surface when walking down a dark street, going into a deserted carpark, sensing footsteps from behind, hearing a noise in an empty house, withdrawing money from an ATM, or in many other situations. Women of all ages, from all walks of life, are attacked in their homes, on the streets, in parks, at work, on public transport, in social settings—it happens everywhere, from the largest city to the most remote farm. There is almost nowhere that a woman can feel totally safe. Worse, women are attacked by people close to them as well as by strangers, acquaintances and workmates. They are often unprepared for attacks by people they know, and their ability to trust, as well as their minds and bodies, can be severely damaged.

Attack can be taken in a broad sense to include all those incidents in which physical force or the threat of it is used or implied. The integral concept here is one of domination, whether it be by intimidation, harassment, grabbing, grappling, punching, kicking or the use of a weapon.

Underlying the threat of violence is the perception that men are physically stronger than women. Social conditioning and personal values allow some males to use and condone physical violence towards women. While the size and strength of men and women vary considerably, it is generally thought that many men have the physical capacity to attack a woman and that most women don't have the strength to fight back. But all the evidence shows that it is not simply a question of strength. More important is the social conditioning that tells men they can treat women this way and tells women they can't fight back.

Research shows that women's safety is most at risk from sexual assault, domestic violence and robbery.

Sexual assault

Most studies show that less than 20% of attacks on women are by strangers. Around 10–15% are by a current or previous partner, up to 30% by other family members, around 10–15% by a friend and around 25% by an acquaintance. A large proportion (up to 70%) of sexual assaults occur in dwellings, many in the woman's own home; often the woman has allowed the attacker to enter, reflecting the high proportion of attackers known to and trusted by women. A significant proportion (over 10%) occur in outdoor areas such as streets, parks and parking areas.[1] It is commonly found that sexual assault is more likely

---

[1] These figures are taken from the report on a phone-in conducted in November 1992 by the NSW Sexual Assault Committee (see bibliography).

to occur in summer; this is found also in police figures on assault and offensive behaviour.[2] This trend may reflect the fact that people socialise more in summer and perhaps drink more alcohol. Police figures also show that sexual assaults are more likely to happen in the evening (about 60–80% between 6pm–6am) than in the day, with a higher percentage occurring on Fridays and Saturdays.

The highest risk adult age groups are women aged 16–20 years, followed by those of 21–25 years. Children aged 10–15 years are also in a high risk group. The risk for age groups over 40 years is much lower. Approximately 75% of attacks involve one male assailant while about 16% involve more than one.[3] Police figures indicate higher than average rates of offending by men aged 18–40, with a peak at about 21–30 years of age.[4] (Note though that police figures reflect reported assaults and represent only a small proportion of crimes.)

While serious physical injury is not typical of sexual assault in Australia, threat, intimidation and physical force were used in most incidents. Around 80% of assailants used physical force and over 50% threatened the woman with physical harm. Extreme physical violence or the presence of weapons was not a significant factor in most cases. Weapons are present in around 10% of cases, although one study indicated that about 20% of assailants *threatened* to use a weapon as part of their intimidation tactics. 'Many women attacked by people with weapons do escape' (Groves & Caignon: 1989, p. 150).

DOMESTIC VIOLENCE

While significant proportions of the community believe that domestic violence is acceptable it will remain difficult for women to bring the problem into the open. There is a feeling that the

2 *Crime and Justice Bulletin*, no. 20, July 1993.

3 NSW Health Department, *Victims of Sexual Assault*, 1993, p. 10.

4 *Crime and Justice Bulletin*, no. 20, July 1993.

home is a private domain, and a sense of shame in letting people know you are experiencing this kind of violence. Like sexual assault, domestic violence is a hidden and under-reported crime.

A clear-cut solution is not always apparent for women who experience violence in their personal relationships. Domestic violence occurs in often complex situations involving patterns of behaviour learned in childhood, other experiences of violence, poor self-image, low financial resources, drinking, drug and psychological problems, and feelings of powerlessness. Violence often begins early in the relationship and continues over a period of time. As well as physical damage, it can damage a woman's self-esteem, reducing her confidence and her ability to make decisions that protect her safety. Children's needs and financial matters can complicate the situation. Many women do not have independent means of support or accommodation.

Overseas research indicates that as many as one in three partnerships involve violence at some stage. At the extreme end of the scale, domestic violence becomes murder. '48% of women but only 9% of men killed in NSW between 1968 and 1986 were killed by their spouse or de facto spouse. In terms of raw numbers, there were three times as many women as men killed by a spouse or de facto spouse.' (Matka: 1991)

Some people ask why women don't simply leave their violent partners, without realising that it is not so easy. Furthermore, many cases of domestic violence occur between couples who are separated, so leaving does not necessarily stop the violence.

Making a decision to get help is a step towards taking control. Some areas now have Domestic Violence hotlines and other agencies which can provide advice and support. If you know someone who is in a violent relationship, listen without jumping to conclusions so they can share their feelings and experiences with you. Getting these things out may enable them to realise they need help. Offer non-judgmental support so that they can discover the best course of action for themselves. Encourage them to seek professional assistance. Reassure them that this is a common problem and their safety is more important than feeling embarrassed, self-conscious or guilty about such a situation.

No matter what has happened up to now, every person has the power to make new choices and to change their own behaviour from this point onwards. We cannot directly change other people's behaviour, but we can change our own and this can give us the power to change our lives. We can change the way we express ourselves and the way we respond to others, both verbally and physically. As a result of our changes, sometimes the people around us change too. But the more we focus on them and their behaviour, the less likely we are to change anything.

Through bringing the problem of domestic violence into the open we can help to create change. When concerted public attention has been focused on particular crime problems—for example, drink driving—it has resulted in reducing offending, partly by highlighting that this kind of behaviour is dangerous and unacceptable.

How RELEVANT ARE STATISTICS?

A recent report stated that:

- One in three girls and one in nine boys will experience some form of sexual assault during their childhood.
- Based on a 1:3 reporting rate, a woman in New South Wales has a one in eight chance of being raped. (Many studies put the reporting rate at between 1:4 and 1:20 which significantly raises the probability of attack.)
- Ten to fourteen per cent of all married women have been or will be raped by their spouse.[1]

Upward trends have been noted in police records of sexual assault and domestic violence in recent years, yet we must be careful about assuming that the actual incidence is increasing.

---

1 NSW Sexual Assault Phone-In Report, November 1992, p. 13.

It may simply be that people are reporting them more. Among the most under-reported of all crimes are those of violence towards women. So the figures we hear represent only a small proportion. However we interpret statistics, women continue to be attacked; for most women it is the *possibility* rather than the probability of sexual assault that is frightening.

Too often, the resulting message for women from statistics on violence is one of fear and powerlessness. This is compounded by sensational reporting of violence which often gives the impression that nothing can be done about these crimes. And yet there are many positive messages that could be given. Numerous studies have shown that if women fight back effectively they have a very good chance of getting away and being safe. In one survey nearly half the women resisted the attack by shouting, calling for help, running away and fighting back.

These success stories are a crucial missing link in most media coverage of violence to women. Women do resist, defuse, fight back and get away more frequently than we realise. But it isn't considered important news and often goes unreported. Such information could provide a counterbalance to all the negative messages presented. Positive information about women who resist makes other women feel empowered. Look for the tiny items buried in remote corners of the newspaper— 'Schoolgirl kicks attacker in shins and escapes', 'Female jogger hits assailant with dog leash'.

One notorious rapist who terrorised women in their homes over a long period of time was chased out of the house on more than one occasion. This was not reported in the media although enormous coverage was given each time he completed another attack. The police also knew that women had resisted these attacks effectively but did not release this information to the community.

This example silently reinforces a common message telling women not to fight back for fear of inviting more injury. But much evidence shows that resisting gives a far greater chance of stopping the attack and getting away safely. Two surveys by the US National Centre for Prevention and Control of Rape have shown that women who resisted were more successful in avoiding rape and physical injury. Sixty per cent of women studied had escaped rape, mostly by fighting back! Both studies concluded that passive victims had a greater risk of serious injury.

While on the one hand women are often told not to fight back, on the other many courts require evidence of resistance to 'prove' lack of consent. Absence of injuries can be interpreted as consent and is one of the reasons police classify a report as unfounded. If the case does go to court, absence of injury can be a major reason for dismissal of the charge. Women who have resisted to the best of their ability may be in better shape to deal with the aftermath than those who later wish they had fought back. Some women feel a sense of regret, a feeling that they may have been able to prevent the attack if they had resisted.

Information about how women prevent attacks tells other women that they can do it too. I recommend to every woman an excellent book called *Her Wits About Her: Self-Defense Success Stories by Women* edited by Gail Groves and Denise Caignon. It contains numerous stories by women from all walks of life about how they successfully dealt with being attacked. It is inspiring to read of their courage and helpful to know about the various strategies they used. Some of them got away from gangs and armed attackers.

There are many statistics we can only guess at—statistics which would tell how many women avoid situations of danger and protect themselves in a variety of ways. Think of this next time you read or hear another negative story about violence to women. Most studies don't ask women about successful resistance. Ask among your friends and you may be surprised how many women have their own success story. Keep in mind that women sometimes don't realise theirs is a success story—despite the fact that they have escaped sexual assault, injury and in some cases death, there is strong social pressure to internalise guilt and blame, and for some women this obscures the positive energy they have used to protect their safety.

I had never thought of this as successful resistance. I was beaten up. It hurt and I was afraid. But now I think of how I wasn't raped. I wasn't killed. I didn't give up. (Groves & Caignon: 1989, p. 102)

How do *you* cope?

The main way in which women cope with the threat of violence is by restricting their activities. Most women have some kind of safety plan, a set of personal dos and don'ts which may operate at a conscious or subconscious level. For example, I feel safe walking here, but not there; I go out in daylight, but not at night; I travel by bus, but not by train. Spend a moment thinking about your approach. When we hear of yet another attack, relevant details are incorporated into our safety plan. And then there is the lurking fear of events we can't anticipate. How can our safety plan cover everything?

•What if my car breaks down in the middle of nowhere?
•What if I'm home alone and hear someone trying to break in?
•What if I arrive home and think there might be an intruder in the house?
•What if I hear footsteps following me into a deserted street or carpark?
•What if I'm attacked while holding my baby or child?

These situations and others raise the uncomfortable possibility that no amount of personal restriction can make a woman feel safe.

In this book my major focus is to help women improve their safety right now. I touch briefly upon the broader issues to provide a backdrop to women's ability to look after themselves and to encourage all genuine work on reducing violence. Real self-confidence is based on the belief that you are worth protecting and the knowledge that you can resist attack and win. This brings inner strength and new opportunities as well as a feeling of safety. Women can take power into their own hands and lives by saying: No matter what happens, I'll do my best. I'll be a survivor, not a victim.

Chapter 2

THE MINDSET AND BODY LANGUAGE OF A SURVIVOR

Our education system places great emphasis on verbal and written communication but little attention is given to non-verbal communication, which we learn informally. Body language is constantly modelled and taught to us as children by everyone around us, with little conscious thought given to the messages being sent and received. Body language is spoken and understood every day. It shows us a lot about power relations between men and women.

All forms of violence are aspects of body language: they are extreme methods of physical communication. Understanding body language is vital for women who want to develop greater personal power and reduce the likelihood of being attacked.

This chapter will show you how to become more aware of the messages you are sending, how to read an attacker's body language and how to maximise the effectiveness of your responses to threatening situations.

Body language covers a vast area, including the gestures, posture, movements and positioning of the many different parts of your body. It also includes how to use your voice—its tone, quality, volume, pitch, whether you interrupt or are interrupted, how formal or informal your speech and manner are, and how familiar or unfamiliar your behaviour is.

Compare the messages being sent in these two photos: left, head down, no eye-contact, shoulders slumped, hands behind back, compared with right, head up, eye contact, posture upright, closest hand providing a barrier, ready for defence or attack.

Feelings are the universal alphabet of body language. Studies show that people from different cultures can instantly recognise emotions without any need for spoken language. Your face is equipped with numerous muscles that are used in the expression of emotions. Have a look at your own facial expressions to find out how your feelings are expressed.

We hear a lot about the differences between men and women, and debate rages over whether such differences are learned or innate. Many so-called gender differences are actually power differences; these are learned socially and can be changed socially. Body language gives us vital clues to the unspoken power relations in our society.

Women and children are bombarded with many similar guidelines about what they can and can't do with their bodies. Some examples are: don't point, don't touch, sit up straight, don't put your feet up, don't lean back, don't turn the chair around backward, don't stare, don't frown, don't show anger. Both women and children are given messages to smile, that it's OK to cry, to lower their heads and eyes to people in authority. They are shown how to exist in small spaces and learn that their space can readily be taken over. They receive gestures like a touch on the head, a pat on the bottom. These gestures are those of a more powerful person to a subordinate.

Studies show that body language between equals is similar, while between unequals it is quite different. Let's look at some of the differences between people with more and less power.

Dominance	Submission
Stare	Lower eyes, avert gaze, blink
Touch	'Cuddle' into the touch
Interrupt	Stop talking
Crowd another's space	Yield, move away
Frown, look stern	Smile
Point	Obey, stop talk or action, move in pointed direction
Familiar address	Polite, more formal address
Head up	Head down
Shoulders square	Shoulders turned away or pulled in
Ignore	Respond
Tower over	Cower under
Standing	Sitting, lying down
Concealed	Exposed
Impassive demeanour	Expressive demeanour

It is interesting to note how many of the dominance signals are used by attackers and how many of the submission signals are shown by victims.

When women protest against the gestures of dominance—for example, being touched and patted by colleagues at work or by acquaintances at a party—the response is often a put-down like, 'Oh, you're being over-sensitive, I was just being friendly'. When women use some of the dominance gestures, men may misinterpret them as a come-on. Many women feel this way about making eye-contact with men and thus avoid it. A different choice can be to look through, above, beyond the man's eyes rather than lowering yours.

THE 'FIGHT OR FLIGHT' RESPONSE TO STRESS

Being attacked or threatened with violence is a stressful situation, and many experts believe that whenever we experience stress the 'fight or flight' mechanism is activated. This biological and psychological response involves a rapid series of changes in the body that can be extremely helpful in a threatening situation. The nervous system carries signals from the brain to the body warning of perceived danger. Instantaneously, huge reserves of energy become available to assist you.

- The heart rate increases, pumping extra oxygen and nutrients to cells.
- A rise in blood pressure increases circulation and triggers the release of adrenalin and related hormones.
- Hyperventilation increases oxygen intake.
- Sugar and fats spill into the bloodstream to provide fuel for immediate energy.
- More blood is sent to the brain and major muscles.

Your body is designed for survival. With this enormous energy instantly available, both running away and fighting back are useful options; it depends on the situation and you which is preferable. The flight response is a direct survival mechanism— get away from the danger immediately. The response to fight back is often based on an inner sense of self that cries out against being violated, a self that says 'How dare you!'.

These strategies will be explored in Chapters 3, 4 and 5.

YOUR BODY LANGUAGE

When you are confronted by a potential attacker, your body language sends an immediate message to that person made up of many small elements. It tells him how you are feeling and what you are likely to do. Will you fight back, run away, struggle or freeze? Your voice conveys whether you're likely to shout, talk, gasp or be silent.

It is normal for most women to feel frightened in such a situation, so don't suppress your fear or expect to feel none at all. Fear is a natural and healthy response to danger; it can provide you with valuable energy as long as it doesn't stifle your survival responses. It is helpful to recognise the way you react when you feel fear. Do you hold your breath? Does your heart race, your stomach tighten? Do your hands go cold or sweaty?

Look inside yourself and you may find anger as well as fear. How dare this person invade your body and mind! How dare he threaten your safety! This can be a turning point for you. If you don't discover anger, you may find a strong urge for self-protection. When you are attacked your survival is being threatened. Finding your inner strength helps you to use fear constructively. This can result in an outer aura that makes you an unlikely victim.

There is a natural sense of outrage that arises when we are attacked. This is something a woman can use to fuel her defense of herself, to bring her will to the surface. The feeling of being violated sometimes expresses itself as a sudden, explosive response that may surprise the attacker. (Groves & Caignon: 1989, p. 91)

If your body language is strong and confident, you give a clear message that you are not an easy victim. This confidence is based on your faith in yourself: no matter what the attacker says or does you will protect yourself to the best of your ability.

Studies of victimology show that offenders judge their victims in a split second. On a broad level, simply being female may be taken as a sign of vulnerability. On a more subtle level, indicators like posture, eye-contact, facial expression and sense of purpose send out significant messages.

Become more aware of your body language
Practise expressing emotions in the mirror: what does your face convey when you feel frightened, surprised, shocked, angry?

- Run a quick checklist of your body's typical posture: How do you stand? How do you move? When do you hold your head up or lower it? What is your shoulder position—square-on or turned to the side? Tense or relaxed?
- How do you walk? What size steps do you take? How purposefully do you move?
- What typical arm movements and gestures do you use? Do your arms swing freely when you walk? To what extent do you 'claim' the territory around you?
- When do you make eye-contact and when do you avert your gaze? What messages are carried by your eyes?
- How do you react to stress, fear, anger? How does this change your body language?

Deliberately practise the body language indicators of dominance and submission; note how using these signals changes the way you feel and the way others react. Experiment in different situations—on the street, at work, at home, with strangers, with friends. Becoming aware of your own typical messages and responses is a starting point for developing powerful, safe body language.

This exercise will help you identify areas you may wish to change. While practising new body language may not change your deeper emotional responses to danger, it can give you a protective outer layer while you work on the inner feelings. Emotional and muscular responses are like the chicken/egg cycle—practise smiling and you feel happier; practise standing up straight and you feel stronger; practise making eye-contact and you feel more in control; practise facing danger with a confident look and you feel more powerful.

HIS BODY LANGUAGE

Since an attacker is so often an insecure, desperate person, uncertain of himself and his motives, there are openings where a woman can slip in a remark, a gesture—or a fist or a kick, if it comes to that. (Groves & Caignon: 1989, p. xxxiv)

As you become more aware of and comfortable with your own body language, the more attention you can give to messages being sent by the attacker. You can pick up many vital clues. Much of this will come across as a hunch and you may not know exactly what he is doing that conveys his message to you. Tuning in to his wavelength gives you a feel for how he will react to the various strategies you may use. As you read and hear more self-defence success stories, you will notice that many women's responses were based on an intuitive assessment of their attacker. This awareness often guided them instinctively into actions that had a high chance of success.

YOUR INTERACTION WITH THE ATTACKER

There was a point during the confrontation when there was a standoff, a point when I felt, this is the moment and either it's going to happen or it's not. I felt like he was deciding too, and I just thought I should be fearless and act like I belonged there and was in total control. (Groves & Caignon: 1989, pp. 62–3)

Like all forms of communication, body language is a two-way process. Sometimes we don't realise that the other person's body language is a reaction to ours. It is often the more powerful person who 'cues' the other person's behaviour. An attacker using dominance signals usually expects the intended victim to reply with signals of submission.

Be aware that changing your behaviour can bring a variety of responses. These responses may include ignoring, punishment, insult, retaliation and submission. But also keep in mind that the attacker is looking for a victim—if you show that you do not fit that role, but will run, shout, lash out, instead of freezing and submitting, you are already well on your way to safety. 'I am safe because I refused to think of myself as his victim,' said one woman who was followed in a deserted railway station and got away using verbal tactics. (Groves & Caignon: 1989, p. 80)

In threatening situations, some of the key factors you can assess are:

The attacker

- How does he present? What messages are you picking up?
- What is your perception of the danger level?
- Does he want money and valuables or do you sense a threat of personal or sexual violence?
- Is he under the influence of drugs or alcohol, is he mentally unbalanced? If so, escaping becomes a high priority because verbal and fighting skills may not get the message across to a person in this condition.
- Is he armed? If so, what with and how is he holding the weapon? This gives you an idea of whether and how he may use it.

You

- What sort of messages are you projecting?
- How can you replace any signals of vulnerability with strength and determination?
- What survival strategies can you use right now?
- Are you likely to get help from anyone else?
- Is there anything you can use as a self-defence weapon?

How to face an attacker

- Establish eye-contact. This has a two-way effect: firstly to pick up his intentions at the earliest opportunity and secondly to project your message to him.
- Keep watching him closely even if you are pretending to be casual. You can pick up many indicators of how he feels and what he is likely to do, as well as getting a description of him.
- Project inner calm; look and feel mentally strong; convey a firm, unruffled image (unless you have chosen other strategies—e.g. shouting, showing your anger, feigning acquiescence).
- Breathe steadily; fear often affects the way you breathe. Getting in touch with your breathing can have a calming effect: it helps to keep your chest open, your muscles relaxed and your mind focused, and it provides the oxygen you need for whatever action you choose.
- Modify your posture: relax your shoulders, keep your body

Face an attacker front-on—do not turn away or let him get behind you.

straight in a natural way, stand in a balanced position with your knees slightly bent and feet shoulder-width apart, ready for action. Keep your hands up in front of your body.

•Regulate the way you speak to use the most effective tone of voice for this situation.

It may be interesting to try some role plays with friends to discover what different responses different tones of voice can generate.

BECOMING MORE ASSERTIVE

Examining your body language and underlying feelings is a step towards discovering how assertive you are. Learning and practising assertive habits in every part of your life is a vital step towards becoming safer. This helps you get in touch with your real needs and enables you to feel more in control of every situation.

Take a look at how you handle difficult situations in your life:

•Do you avoid confrontation?
•Do you rely on other people to sort out problems?
•How do you respond to situations you don't like?

- Are you able to express how you feel and what you want in these situations?
- Are you able to remain firm on what you want or do you give way when someone opposes you?
- Do you say yes when you really mean no?
- Do you smile when you are angry or upset?
- Do you apologise or feel guilty for feeling angry?

Many writers in the area of personal protection suggest that women undertake a course in assertiveness training. They point out that if your usual reaction to life is passive, your response to being attacked may mirror this.

Chapter 3

SAFETY STRATEGIES

One of the most surprising aspects of these calls [to the rape hotline] was the fact that so many women got away without being raped. Over the years a consistent picture began to emerge of women effectively resisting, paying attention to clues about a potential attack and escaping by many different means. (Groves & Caignon: 1989, p. xvii)

This chapter presents a wide range of strategies you can use when confronted with danger and shows how you can take control. You will learn that there are many options available. You will discover which strategies you feel most comfortable with, as well as how and when you could use them. These strategies are presented as possible choices for you to consider. No-one can say what will work and what won't. It is up to you to assess them and focus on those that feel right for you. Exactly what you do and how you do it depends on the particular situation you are in. You will make those decisions instantly, on the spot. The more strategies you feel comfortable using, the safer and more confident you will feel in all situations.

Very few attacks come completely without warning. The vast majority, while usually unexpected, have some kind of lead-up or clues that may help you to organise your responses. A major step towards safety is your initial assessment of the situation. This can be most difficult when being attacked by someone close to you because it may come as a complete shock, and you may disbelieve or deny that it is actually happening. Once you can identify that your safety is under threat and gauge the extent of the danger you are already part way to defending yourself.

> Most women who are attacked remember feeling a hunch, an intuition, a nonverbal perception before something physical happened—the feeling that something is wrong. The sooner women act on this intuition, the more likely they are to be safe in the end . . . This feeling is especially important with people we have reason to trust, but who take advantage of that trust. (Groves & Caignon: 1989, p. xxiii)

Safety strategies fall into two broad categories, avoidance and resistance, and you may use both in the one situation. Avoidance may mean quietly moving away from potential danger before anything happens or it may mean running away from an attack at the earliest opportunity. Resistance includes a wide range of verbal and physical responses. The foundation of both is awareness.

AWARENESS

The first step towards being safe everywhere, at all times, is awareness. Our senses are constantly providing us with a wealth of information that we are not always fully aware of. Tune in to all the messages you are receiving and focus on those that relate to safety. In particular, notice any change from what is safe and normal. Sometimes it is tempting to ignore potential danger in the hope that it will go away, but this may lead you to miss out on vital information and lose time to organise your responses.

When people talk about intuition, a capacity often attributed to women, what they are really talking about is awareness— basically, finely-tuned senses that are taking in all the sounds, sights, movements, feelings and even smells around you. Two of the most obvious senses we can use are our eyes and ears. Looking and listening help greatly in the prevention of danger. The further ahead and afield that we cast these senses, the earlier we can receive vital information. This gives us more choices than are usually available when we suddenly realise that we are already in danger.

Women who are in touch with this channel of information have immense ability to choose the right action at the optimum moment. They are able to observe small changes in the attacker's behaviour, find or create a moment his attention is distracted, see a path of escape at it opens up, notice someone or something nearby that may be of assistance. When you trust your intuition, you are able to respond second by second to the situation, rather than being locked into a single, predetermined reaction; you are able to be more flexible in your responses, and change your actions in response to changes in the attacker's strategy.

Driving to a party one Saturday night, Tanya and Sandra went to a hotel to pick up wine. As they entered the carpark, a group of drunken men came out. A silent voice inside Tanya said, 'Here's potential danger; get out quickly before they notice us.' Sandra didn't receive this message, so she kept going and within seconds was blocked in by another car. Now the men had noticed them, and were starting to crowd around and yell suggestive comments. Sandra became flustered, her driving erratic. Finally she was on the way out, but now they were being followed by two men in a car. Sandra started to panic: 'Tanya, help, do something!' Her voice was high and fast. Tanya quickly assessed the situation: they were safe in their car at this moment. 'Everything's going to be okay. Lock your door, take a deep breath and drive normally. I'll check the directory for the nearest police station.'

- *Forward awareness*—Tanya noticed the first hint of danger and had an instant impulse to get away before being noticed. She acted normally and didn't show fear, especially as there was no immediate threat. Her calm behaviour confirmed that she was in control and enabled her to choose a safe course of action.

- *Delayed awareness*—Sandra moved into a potentially dangerous situation, not noticing the people and circumstances. Fear affected her behaviour in a way that could have been detrimental to their safety. Communicating this fear can confirm the men's power and the women's potential to become victims.

Obviously it is ideal to get away from a situation *before* anything happens. When your senses are fully alert, you notice warning signs and react before there is any actual danger. You can defuse the situation. You exercise power over your own safety. If you can't escape before anything happens, get away at the first possible moment. Maintain awareness and remain as calm as possible so you can find opportunities for escape.

Think ahead to where you are going—if there are substantial risks, consider changing your plans, for example: go somewhere different, go at a different time, use a different mode of transport, take someone with you, ask someone to meet you there.

STAGES OF AN ATTACK

While research shows that a large number of attacks on women are planned, there are also a large number that are classified as 'opportunist'—that is, the attacker takes advantage of a situation as it arises. For example, someone has broken into your home to rob you, but finding you there, decides to attack you as well; or perhaps you are dropped home from a social situation by an acquaintance who attacks you when invited in for coffee. One of the key factors is that the attacker sees you as vulnerable.

Some studies identify a sequence of stages that characterise many attacks. While not all attacks follow this pattern, many include some of these elements:

• The first stage is surveillance and target selection, with emphasis on the vulnerability of the person and the isolation of the environment.

• The second stage is testing the potential victim, usually by making verbal contact, to see whether she can be intimidated or not. It is crucial how a woman responds at this stage, for if you show that you are not a victim and will stand up to the verbal approach (which frequently includes obscene remarks and threats) the attack will often be defused before anything further happens.

- The third stage is where the attacker moves the potential victim to an isolated position (if she is not already in one); at this stage physical contact usually occurs. A woman's confidence and skills in self defence are vital at this point.
- The next stage is the actual attack, which is often accompanied by verbal and physical intimidation. Many women fear they are going to be seriously harmed or even killed.
- In the final stage, the attacker may do and say things to minimise his prospects of being caught, for example, tie up the woman, cut the phone cord, threaten her again.

STRATEGY ONE—RUNNING AWAY, ESCAPING

Running away from an attacker or a dangerous situation can be one of the most sensible options. Don't for a second think that it is 'cowardly'—if it helps you to be safer, it is a life-enhancing decision showing your strength and control.

Factors to consider
- Where are you running to? Is there a safe place nearby? How far is it? Can you make it there quickly? Will it be a truly safe destination?
- Are your shoes suitable for running? If not, can you get them off and run? What is the ground surface like for running?
- Do your clothes enable a swift running action?
- What are you carrying? Will it slow you down? Can you drop something?
- How fit are you? How far and how fast can you run?
- How fit is the attacker? Do you think he can outrun you?

In a split second you can process this information, and a quick glance is all you need to assess the attacker's ability to run. If the answer to one or some of these questions is no, it may be wiser not to run. Don't waste valuable time and energy on a strategy that has a low chance of success. If you run and he catches you, you may have used up energy you could have saved for other options—for example, maintaining your composure and using some of the verbal methods listed below, or standing your ground ready to fight back. You may be exhausted and thus more easily overpowered. You may start to doubt that you will get away.

It is important to maximise the use of both your mental and physical energy.

Examples:

You're walking home down a side street and notice a man leaning against a fence about two metres ahead. He steps out into the path and makes an obscene suggestion, reaching towards you. He looks rather unfit and is not dressed for jogging. You're wearing a loose dress, flat shoes and carrying a light handbag. It's about 100 metres back to a shop on the main road where you know the people well, and know they will help you. You turn and run really fast, quickly glancing behind in case he follows. He is already disappearing down a laneway. You run to the shop, call the police and ring a friend to come and meet you.

If you are approached by an armed attacker, escaping is usually the safest strategy. As Jane came out of the hardware store, she passed a scruffy young man. She heard him behind her talking about her clothes and her body. She turned to face him. From the way he spoke it was clear he was mentally unbalanced. She felt really edgy. Her car was close—could she get to it quickly? Suddenly she noticed that he was holding a screwdriver pointed towards her at about thigh height. At the same instant she realised her briefcase was on that side and would provide some protection if he attacked.

Cautiously she took a couple of steps back, giving no sign she had seen the weapon, and gestured casually across the street behind him. ' Look,' she pointed, 'is that a friend of yours calling?' As he turned to look she ran straight to her car, facing his direction as she got in. He just blended in with the passing traffic on the street. Her heart was pounding as she drove to the police station.

When not to run away

• You have nowhere safe and close to run to.

• Your clothes, shoes, baggage, etc. are not suited to swift movement.

• Your physical condition doesn't allow it—for example, respiratory illness, injury.

• The attacker looks to be fit, strong and a good runner.

Think of running away as an active choice rather than a panic reaction. Train yourself to make choices, with the emphasis on you *acting* rather than reacting. If your action doesn't work—for example, he is catching up—you can change strategy. Don't allow him to gain power; you are in control.

STRATEGY TWO—VERBAL RESPONSES

Your voice is one of your best self-defence weapons. It may be all that is needed to prevent an attack. Your voice can convey more than just words—it tells the attacker by your tone and intensity how much determination and courage you have.

Some women fear they will freeze in the throat and not be able to utter a sound; it is not uncommon to have dreams about this, and it actually does happen to a few people. However, many women who fear voicelessness discover that their voice stays with them—in fact, they are amazed at the instant power their voice can convey when their survival is threatened.

There are many different ways we can use our voices in self defence including: shouting, screaming, talking, threatening and persuading.

When faced with danger, assess the situation instantly—who else is around? Could people hear if you called out? Is there a chance someone may come to your assistance? How nervous does the attacker look? What intentions does he project? Remember that he also is under stress, and his 'fight or flight' mechanism may be activated too.

Is he likely to run away? What sort of person does he seem to be? Do you know him? If so, what do you know about him and the way he is likely to react? If he seems very uncertain and has a clear escape route, he may run away if you use a strong verbal response. Is he likely to try and silence you? If so, how? By putting a hand over your mouth? By striking you? By trying to push you over? Could you still make a lot of noise if he tried to silence you? Be ready to run or fight if this is his response.

One study of sexual assault showed that in approximately a third of cases, there were people within hearing range; shouting could have frightened the attacker away and possibly brought helpers to the scene. One of the important aspects of verbal self defence is to express what you want very clearly and simply, and to keep saying it, undistracted by what the attacker may say. This clear, repeated expression of what you want is a basic tenet of assertive behaviour.

> *An assault is an act of power over another person. To maintain that power, the assailant must effectively dehumanize the woman he is attacking. When the woman simply looks him in the eye and says exactly what she means, sometimes his whole rationale for attacking her begins to crumble.* (Groves & Caignon: 1989, p. xxxvi)

Let's examine some verbal responses.

Shouting
One American study of assaults that were prevented showed that in 60% of cases the women used a loud, clear, sharp yell as part of their response. Your aim may be to scare the attacker away or to attract attention, or both. If it is to attract the attention of people within earshot, remember the results of one study which showed that shouting 'Fire!' brought more response than shouting 'Rape!'. Shouting can convey a strong message both to the attacker and to people who can hear. It can convey anger and active resistance to the attacker. Remember that he does not want to be caught and may flee if you attract attention. Shouting also confirms your strength, reminding you of your own power and expressing your outrage at being put in this position.

As she shouts and gestures strongly towards him, the attacker steps back, placed on the defensive.

If you would like to feel more confident about shouting at an attacker, start to practise. Work out what you would say. Which words and expressions come naturally to you? Experiment with different messages and tones. What gestures would you use to add emphasis to your words? How would your posture be?

Find a place and time where you can practise at full volume. Feel your diaphragm. Discover how you would use your energy and feelings to shout; this can fuel a loud and clear message. If his ear is close to your mouth shouting loudly will hurt him quite a lot and he will probably put his hand over his ear. This can give you more time to escape or resist. Remember:

• *Tone*—firm, strong, possibly aggressive.

• *Volume*—as loud as possible (this in itself might give the attacker enough of a fright to send him running; people are often startled when someone shouts suddenly and loudly).

• *Message*—clear, repeated.

• *Examples*—'Go away!' 'Leave me alone!' 'Stop or you'll get hurt!' 'I'm warning you! Get away from me!' 'Fire! Help! Fire! Fire!' 'Call the police!'

Another idea is to shout out the names of people you know

(even if they are nowhere near), calling for their assistance—for example, 'Dave, Marion, Ken, come and help me get rid of this guy!'

Screaming

I believe that shouting is a more powerful response than screaming. Screaming may convey fear rather than anger and while it is quite natural to feel frightened, it is better not to show this fear to the attacker as he may interpret it as victim behaviour. If fear is accompanied by other non-verbal cues like shrinking or cowering, it may prompt the attacker to try to silence your response.

Put yourself in the attacker's shoes—how would you react if your intended victim screamed? Think about how likely screaming is to bring helpers to the scene. Would it sound like real distress? How often do we investigate screams to see if someone needs help? It is easy to ignore it and say: 'I don't want to get involved', 'It's probably a domestic, they'll sort it out', 'It's just kids playing'.

Can you use a scream to convey a strong 'Go away' message? If you believe screaming is a useful option for you, think about how you would do it and what you would say. Practise making the sound lower down from your diaphragm rather than your throat.

Talking

Normal speech   If approached by an attacker, consider the possibility of talking in a 'normal' tone and manner. You might say something like: 'What are you doing?' 'What do you want?' What you say depends on the specific situation and what they have said or done to you. Think about how you could use normal speech to deter an attacker. In situations when the attacker is not overtly threatening, some women have avoided an attack by pretending that it is a 'normal' situation and using conversation to defuse the attacker's intentions.

One possible approach is to get the attacker talking about something of interest or concern to him—perhaps his family, his goals, his hobbies. This may enable you to verbally redirect

When an attacker approached this woman, she decided to take control of the situation verbally by asking him the time before he could say anything. She didn't show fear.

his attack. Another approach is to speak in a firm, assertive manner, telling him what you want him to do:

> 'You turn around and get right back on that train,' I told him. 'I know this isn't your stop, so you'd better leave me alone.' (Groves & Caignon: 1989, p. 73)

> I looked him in the eye. 'You don't belong in here, this is a women's bathroom and you need to get out.' I kept repeating the same thing. And I pushed him to the side, stepped past him and walked out. (ibid, pp. 62–3)

Praise, humour   Is there anything at all you could praise the attacker for? It could be part of an overall plan you have of playing for time and getting to safety. This may be so unexpected that it confuses him. If it is someone you know, you may appeal to his good points. Praise is recognised as an effective way of changing people's behaviour. In an attack situation, it is not the first strategy that will usually come to mind, but there may be a few situations where it could work.

While humour is probably the last thing on your mind, think about how it might disarm your attacker. The overriding message would be that you are not a victim because you don't show fear. If you are the sort of person who can use this response in other difficult situations, humour may be an option for you.

Distraction   Talk to distract the person, to give yourself more time to run or fight or get to a better location. You might say something like: 'Did you drop something over there? Is that a wallet on the ground?' Or see if you can get him talking about something else.

Act insane   Speak and behave in a way that is completely ridiculous—start jabbering nonsense sounds or saying crazy sentences, accompanied by appropriate gestures. The purpose of this is to deter the attacker. I rate it quite low in the whole scheme of strategies, but it may be the right choice for some people or situations.

Emphasise that you are not the victim they want   Choose messages that have a strong deterrent value—for example, that you have AIDS, that you are prone to violent epilepsy when under stress and can feel an attack coming on right now (start shaking and waving your arms around).

THREATENING

In one study some attackers reported that threat could deter them. Use a very strong tone and quality of voice, probably with an undercurrent of aggression. Put a snarl on your face and use threatening gestures as you describe what is going to happen to them. For example—'I'm going to demolish you. If I were you I'd try to get away now while you're still in one piece' or 'I go wild when someone tries to harm me, I can't control myself. You'll get really hurt.'

If you can imagine yourself threatening an attacker, think about what you would say. Practise saying it in a safe, secluded place and notice what it feels like to speak this way. Does it empower you? What facial expressions and gestures come with the words and feelings? If you know the attacker, would you threaten to tell everyone about his behaviour?

PERSUASION, PLEADING

Earlier we saw that pleading was associated with an attack being completed rather than being stopped. I am dubious about the value of persuasion except as an interim strategy because its underlying message is one of powerlessness, confirming what the attacker wants. However, here's one example of clever deception I read about: A woman was attacked in her own home by a would-be rapist armed with a knife. She was terrified. She said 'Please—I'm so scared—I'll do anything you want, only please, put the knife down'. She gave the impression that she was defenceless and acquiescent. He put the knife down. She ran out of the room, locked him in and called the police.

In other situations women have used this strategy to get themselves into a better location—for example, if approached in a park, pretend to acquiesce, mention how uncomfortable it will be and invite the attacker somewhere else, where you will have more options. If persuasion sounds useful for you, it would be important to assess the attacker. What clues are there that he may respond to this approach? Do you have a back-up plan if it doesn't work? Formulate some examples of what you would say.

MATCHING BODY LANGUAGE

What you want to project depends on which of the approaches you choose. If you shout and show your anger, you may also gesture vigorously, for example, a sweep of your arm as you yell 'Get away!'. If you threaten the attacker, you may also point vigorously with your finger for emphasis. If you act crazy, you may make weird faces. If you pretend to go along with it until the best moment for action, you may deliberately look a little powerless—lower your head slightly, use a soft tone of voice.

Think back to the basics of body language, and for most verbal responses focus on how to convey an impression of power. Stand up straight yet relaxed, face front-on, keep your shoulders square, hands up near your face, maintain eye-contact, as the woman is doing in the photo on page 18.

If your verbal response doesn't deter the attacker he may attack you immediately. If your hands are up, you can react quickly both to protect yourself and to strike him. But if your hands are behind your back, in your pockets, down at your sides, you may lose valuable time in stopping his attack. Find a position for your hands that is natural for you, for example, touch an earring, place your hand on your chin, position your hands in front of your body.

Once you are attacked, the sooner you react the safer you can be. The longer your reaction takes the greater your chance of being hurt. Stand in an easy comfortable position with your feet about shoulder-width apart so that you feel stable. Keep your legs relaxed and your knees slightly bent—this enhances both balance and mobility. With your knees slightly bent, every physical reaction is easier for you, be it running away, kicking or moving in response to the attack.

Experiment to find a standing position that enables you to move easily and feel well balanced. The more stable you feel, the better you will cope with various surfaces—for example, on a slope, steps, rough uneven ground or with high heels on.

BE READY FOR ACTION

Regardless of which verbal approaches you believe you would use, do not rely completely on them; be ready to change strategy as soon as you see your first approach is not working. Be ready to protect yourself, be ready to escape.

Chapter 4

FIGHTING BACK

Your knowledge that you can fight back projects a very powerful message to your attacker—it tells him he has chosen to attack the wrong person. Skill and the confidence that you can fight back often provide the ultimate deterrent. You look and act in a manner that mean you probably will not be attacked. The more self-defence ability you have, the stronger your body language is in preventing attack.

Sociologists have found that women who fight back get away more often than women who are passive. They note that pleading with the attacker and acting passively seem to increase the chance that a rape will be completed. The more strategies a woman is able to use—including yelling, fleeing, reasoning and fighting back—the more likely she is to escape with minimal injuries. (Groves & Caignon: 1989, p. xxiii)

Skill can overcome brute strength. This chapter covers a number of simple but cleverly designed physical responses to attacks. All the techniques fit together in a systematic way so that you don't have to memorise an endless variety of complicated moves. The movements are easy to learn and to apply for women of any age, regardless of size, strength or fitness level. The emphasis is on helping you to discover your own capacities for survival and self-empowerment.

While it can be beneficial to do a women's self-defence course, this book is based on the belief that even without training, women are capable of fighting back and winning.

Key points

• Practise forward planning and awareness.

• Develop assertive body language, minimise submissive behaviour.

• Get in touch with your survival instincts, identify your anger as well as your fear; this can provide the mental and physical energy you need to fight back.

• React when you have the chance.

• Study the fighting techniques shown here; file away in your mind those that would work best for you.

Naturally, proper training will enhance your ability to fight back. Readers who want to practise and consolidate these skills are advised to go through the moves shown in the Tool Box on pages 50–8 alone and with a partner; try out the different attack responses shown throughout the book. Remember that practising with friends is different from a real situation because your survival isn't threatened, so you don't have the adrenalin and determination that will aid you if you are attacked; you will also be holding back because you don't want to hurt your friend.

Simply reading, absorbing and implanting these moves in your mind will give you a good chance of using them if the need arises. Often all a woman needs to harness her natural ability to fight back is to see, read or hear about simple, effective ways to use her body, like those shown here. I believe that the 'fight or flight' reaction to stress is a strong part of our makeup. Knowing how this works, even on a simple level, can give you a better chance. The various physiological reactions that occur when you experience stress can all give you more energy to fight back—for example, the rush of adrenalin, increased blood flow to the big muscles, rapid breathing supplying extra oxygen to the blood.

FIGHTING BACK

The fighting methods described and shown in this chapter and the next have been developed and simplified over sixteen years of studying and teaching Wing Chun. This Chinese system of Kung Fu is widely recognised as one of the most simple and practical of the self-defence arts. Much of my teaching has concentrated on short courses for women. In some situations a 'short' course has meant just one lesson, so I have learnt to eliminate anything that is complex or difficult. I have streamlined my knowledge, retaining a basic set of the most effective, easily-learnt movements.

Once women discover the emotional strength to resist attack and are shown a clever approach to fighting back, it becomes clear that they can defend themselves very effectively. Although most men are bigger and stronger than women, they have many vulnerable targets, and women have many 'weapons' they can use.

Physically fighting back is generally one of the last choices for most women, except for those who are well-trained in an instinctive form of self defence or those who find it easy to strike out for self-protection. Most women have had little or no experience of hitting people, and such reactions do not come easily to them. Those women who have grown up with childhood play-fighting may find it easier to imagine themselves fighting back, although social conditioning and learning to be a 'lady' may have taken the edge off these skills.

There are many women with no experience of fighting, however, who have successfully defended themselves, the strength and clarity of their survival instinct prompting them into immediate action.

Proper forms of self defence focus on how to stop yourself from being hurt. Part of this may involve striking the attacker with as much force as is necessary to stop him. This is not violence, it is preventing violence. If you can't get away or stop him, more harm will probably occur.

Many women don't like the thought of hurting people, and this can be a barrier to fighting back. I believe that learning to defend yourself has nothing to do with wanting to hurt people—it is the opposite. If you abhor violence, you need to know how to stop it. Knowing how to defend yourself often means you can prevent violence.

If you feel that your dislike of hurting someone may stop you from defending yourself, try a few visualisations—imagine how you might feel when attacked. What if your children, your mother, a friend, someone elderly, was threatened? It is one thing to believe in non-violence and minimise any physical harm that you have control over, but it is another thing altogether to allow violence to yourself or other innocent victims to go unchecked.

Where do you stand legally?

The law on assault states that you are within your rights to use a 'reasonable' amount of force if you believe that you are in danger and that the person threatening you can actually carry through with the threat. You don't have to wait to be hit before you use self defence if you honestly believe that the person is about to harm you—you can react before they touch you. Commonsense provides a guideline for what is 'reasonable' force.

Examples: You are at a party with friends and a mutual acquaintance starts hassling and groping you. A palm strike to the shoulders to send him backwards, combined with a verbal warning, is probably 'reasonable'. Only his pride and balance have been injured.

By contrast, you are in a dark deserted street late at night, and someone jumps out threatening you with a knife. You cannot run away and fear for your life. He says he will kill you. You manage to control the knife, kick his knee with a low heel kick and knock him to the ground with several punches. This response is probably 'reasonable'.

All the responses to attacks in this book follow a sensible interpretation of the law on assault, showing actions that use a 'reasonable' amount of force. You can modify the amount of force you use for each movement according to the level of danger. For example, a low heel kick may on the one extreme break the attacker's knee, while in a minor situation it may just be used to lightly bruise his shin as a warning.

When fighting back is the only option

In some cases you do not have the choice of running away or talking yourself out of danger.

• What if you are trapped in a room or a lift, cornered in a carpark or house, or if you have a child with you?

• What if the attacker is not deterred by other responses?

• What if the attacker strikes or grabs you immediately, before you have a chance to run or talk?

It is useful to be ready to fight back at any moment. In a minority of cases an attack comes completely without warning. This is when you really need instinctive physical self-protection skills that happen by reflex.

Many women successfully fight back. Often the attacker runs away when a woman fights back because he was looking for a victim but found a fighter, someone who might harm him rather than allow him to harm her. If a woman shows her determination to fight back the attacker may flee before anything has happened because he can read her body language.

In many cases, once the woman shows she will fight back, the attacker's manner changes to one of fear and submission. Many attackers are cowardly people seeking desperately to gain a sense of power by dominating someone whom they see as even more powerless than they are. Otherwise why would they pick on people smaller than themselves?

> . . . he just lunged at me . . . I was wearing a skirt and heels and makeup, so I'm sure he thought that I was an easy mark and had no idea what he was getting into. I hit him in the chest to back him off so he wouldn't grab me. I assumed that I was going to have to really take him out because we were trapped in a little tiny elevator. But he backed right off and said, 'I'm sorry, I'm sorry, don't hit me'. I kept looking at him, thinking, You make one move and I'm going to really have to hurt you . . .
> (Groves & Caignon: 1989, p. 212)

THE BEST MOVES——A STRATEGIC SYSTEM

Outlined here are a series of key techniques that are easy to use and really work. These movements form a simple integrated system, rather than the ad hoc collection found in many books and courses. The main benefit of this is that the moves are like Lego pieces—they all fit together, and with a small number of parts you can create a wide range of applications to cover many situations. Because the movements are systematically connected you don't have to learn and memorise dozens of complicated patterns. You have a much better chance of reacting immediately by reflex. This is one of the keys to successful self defence. A simple Tool Box containing the essential movements for your protection is shown, as well as how to apply them in common attack situations. These basic moves can be used over and over again.

Key features of effective self defence

- simplicity
- ease of learning
- directness
- practicality
- power
- reflex
- using the attacker's force against him

Simplicity   All these movements are based on natural body actions so you don't need any special qualities of fitness, flexibility, coordination or strength to make them work. The movements have been streamlined so that every woman can use them.

Ease of learning   Because the moves are simple and natural, women of any size or age can learn them quickly and easily. When you are attacked you don't usually have time to recall long complicated manoeuvres. These small, economical movements require the minimum of effort and energy.

Directness   Built into the design of this system is immediate counter-attack: as soon as the attacker physically threatens you, these responses enable you to strike him and defend yourself simultaneously. This has the instant effect of turning the tables on him when he least expects it. It often means that you only need to use *one* movement—a counter-attack—rather than trying to defend first and then attack. If you can only defend, the person may keep attacking you. Counter-attack gives you the upper hand. *The surprise element of this is very powerful—it is probably the last thing the attacker expects, therefore he is vulnerable and unlikely to be able to stop your counter-attack.*

Practicality   These movements can be used regardless of the clothing you are wearing or your physical surroundings. Be wary of self-defence movements that would only work if you had loose clothes on or a lot of room around you. You may be wearing tight clothing or be in a cramped space.

Power   These movements can be used effectively against a bigger person. They show how to overcome the attacker's strength by using deflection, redirection and leverage rather than by trying to use your (possibly lesser) strength against him. This method teaches you to use *structures* of your body that are naturally strong to counter an attack, rather than individual muscles or muscle groups that may not be strong enough. In addition, this system focuses on using the strong parts of your body to attack his weak or vulnerable points—for example, use your heel to his knee, the heel of your palm or your elbow to his jaw or solar plexus. It also teaches you to maximise the use of your whole body mass rather than only using part. Simple concepts like continuous punching mean that you can quickly deliver many blows to the one spot. So, even if your single punch isn't a knockout, four or six of them to one vulnerable point can have a major impact.

Reflex   Built into this system is the concept of reacting immediately the attacker makes a threatening move. By reacting straight away, especially with a counter-attack, you maximise the surprise element and prevent him from getting a hold on you; you can probably stop the attack before he has harmed you. Simple, direct, relaxed movements enhance the speed of your reflexes.

Using the attacker's force against him   Another inbuilt advantage derived, like many here, from the clever strategies of Wing Chun, is using the attacker's force against him rather than struggling or fighting force with force. Learning to relax and keeping your balance are important. For example—when you are pulled forward, keep your body as one and go with the force of the pull, using his force as well as your own to hit him. See the photos on page 65. Similarly, if he pushes you, go with the force rather than trying to push back; as you turn and redirect (somewhat like a revolving door) you use his push combined with your strike to have more impact. See page 64.

ASSESSING SELF-DEFENCE COURSES

These seven key features can be used to assess the effectiveness of any self-defence course you may think about joining. Take into account also the following limiting factors:

Instructor's attitude   The instructor may hold stereotyped and negative views of women and their ability in this field. Assess the instructor's approach, attitudes and training methods; learn from a woman if possible—she can be a good role model.

Complicated, lengthy sequences   Anything that takes too much time and movement before you can strike, control or escape from the attacker is of questionable value (for example, five manoeuvres to get out of a throat grab—you may have stopped breathing by then). The attacker won't just stand there cooperating while you perform several preliminary moves. Look for systems like Wing Chun that feature fast, direct counter-attack.

Difficult moves   If special abilities are required for particular moves, like a high level of coordination, agility, fitness or acrobatic skill, many women will not be able to learn and use those moves (for example, a reverse spinning kick to the head, a jumping front kick).

The need for strength   Most methods of self defence are limited by this factor, apart from those based on a system like Wing Chun. Look at how strenuous the movements are: do they require a lot of strength to make them work? Do they teach you to meet force with force, using blocking rather than redirection? Analyse the moves and try them out against someone stronger than you. Do they work? The special feature of direct counter-attack shown in this book further minimises the need for you to be strong; hitting the attacker immediately will often halt his attack.

To sum up, in assessing a self-defence course ask yourself:

•How practical are the movements?

•How quickly can they be learnt and used?

•Could I do what is shown?

•How confident do I feel that the moves would work against someone stronger?

•Do I feel comfortable in this learning environment?

If the answers to any of these questions are negative, look for another course.

PERSONAL ALARMS AND OTHER DEVICES

In this book I frequently mention the idea of carrying something useful for defence. What I have in mind are everyday items like an umbrella or a walking stick that can be used as extensions to your arms to counter-attack an assailant, especially if he is armed with a knife.

Some women consider deliberately carrying a device to assist them in self defence; examples I have heard of include using hairspray or aerosol deodorant to spray an attacker's face. One woman who was attacked in a deserted laundromat deterred her attacker by spraying pre-wash cleanser into his eyes. From a legal point of view, you must have a lawful purpose for any object you are carrying. But having a device doesn't mean you will be able to use it or that it will be effective. (A US study showed that tear gas sprayed in the face did not stop a determined attacker from advancing.) If the device is in your bag, you may not have time to get it out when you need it. Both the accuracy and the range required for these things are far greater than for your own physical skills such as a punch, kick, elbow or palm strike.

Recently several personal alarms have come onto the market. Even if the alarm is in your hand, you may not be able to use it as quickly as your skills in fighting back. If it is very loud, it may scare the attacker away, but do you think it will bring helpers to the scene? Think of the numerous car and building alarms we hear daily and ignore.

I believe that the most reliable and effective forms of self defence are those that are part of you: your legs and wits for escaping; your voice; your body for fighting back.

If it makes you feel safer to carry something for which you have a lawful purpose as well as its defence purpose, then do so. However, be aware of the limitations and do not fall into the trap of thinking it will do the job by itself. Real safety and power come from your own inner confidence, determination and will to survive, rather than from any device.

Chapter 5

Your Tool Box for effective self defence

In this chapter and Chapter 6 a variety of self-defence movements are shown in different situations of attack. Most of them are drawn from the collection of simple movements outlined in this chapter—what I call your Tool Box for self defence. These movements are guidelines for you to use as they best suit you. There may be other ways of using the movements than described here—for example, if you're sitting or lying down, the target for your punch or elbow strike may be the groin rather than the jaw (see page 65). Adapt the movements to suit yourself.

The centre line

Imagine a vertical line running down the centre front of the body—many vulnerable points are located along this line. These are effective striking targets on the opponent, and areas of your body you must protect.

Face the attacker front-on

This gives you both a physical and a psychological advantage. Physically it means that you can use either arm for defence or attack, you can use them simultaneously, you can use either leg, you can use one arm and one leg combined, or even both arms at the same time as kicking him. The possibilities are far greater than if you are side on. Being front-on also means you can use your whole body mass to generate power. If you are

44

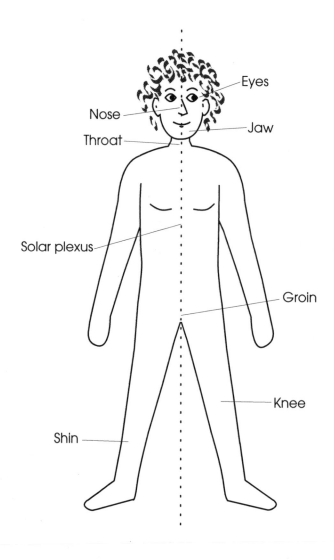

The centre line of the body is the most vulnerable to attack—remember this for both defence and attack.

attacked from the side or behind, try to turn front-on if you can. If this isn't possible there are still many effective responses you can use.

Shortest distance, quickest strikes

Once you face the attacker front-on, the path from your centre line to his body indicates the shortest distance for your strikes. You can hit him very quickly, usually without warning. There is no need to draw your arm or leg back before striking; this could telegraph your intention and give him extra time to try and stop you. With your hands at the centre line, both defending and attacking require only a small amount of time and movement.

Hit him where it hurts and protect yourself at the same time

Your strikes start from your own centre and aim to his centre, simultaneously guarding you and hitting him where it will have real impact.

Maximise your power

Striking from your centre means you can use your whole body mass more than if your strike comes from the side of your body. Imagine a car has broken down and you have to push it—most power can be generated if you put the arms to the centre of your body and your whole weight behind them.

PROTECT YOUR PERSONAL SPACE

When someone tries to attack you, they are moving into the body-language zone usually reserved for intimate contact. Experiment and discover where the boundaries of your personal zone are. Here are some guidelines:
• Imagine a firm plastic bubble around you that encircles your intimate zone.

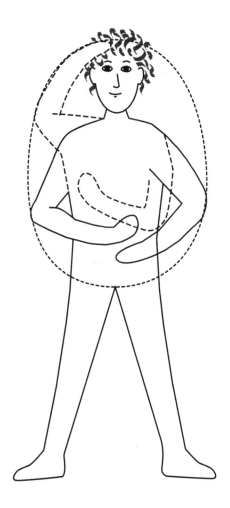

Your imaginary bubble protects your most vulnerable areas—the defensive movements of your arms help to define this space.

•Use your arms at their optimum angle to protect this zone. The structural power of your arm(s) moving at this angle acts as a redirecting force—like water flowing off the plastic bubble, this shape in your arm can divert incoming force away from you. You will notice this angle frequently mentioned and shown throughout. Don't be too worried about the technical aspects (for example, the exact measurement of the angle—is it 105 degrees or 115?); a better guideline is to experiment and find the position that feels strongest for you.

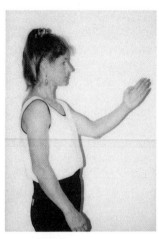

Right: The approximate shape of your optimum angle

Below left: Both arms in optimum angle position...

Below right: ... can be raised to guard the whole upper body.

• Your arms and legs are used for striking as well as redirecting; hitting immediately can keep the attacker outside your personal zone altogether. If you use a strike to stop him from advancing he can't get close enough to harm you and may be deterred by this first response.

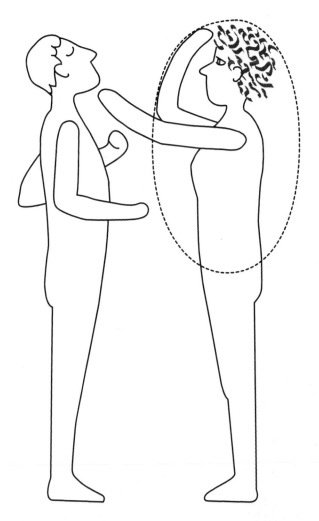

While your defending arm deflects any blow and protects your space, your other arm can strike out beyond the bubble to attack.

Your Tool Box

One simple way of classifying your movements is for attacks from the front, side or behind. Note how much of our self defence is actually counter-attacking our assailant.

Attacks from the front

COUNTER-ATTACKS WITH YOUR LEGS

Low heel kick Thrust your heel forward to the centre with your toes pulled back, and aim to the shin, knee, groin or midsection. Remember what it's like to bump your leg on a drawer or a towbar? It can really hurt. No matter how strong the attacker is, his knee and shin are not protected by his bulk.

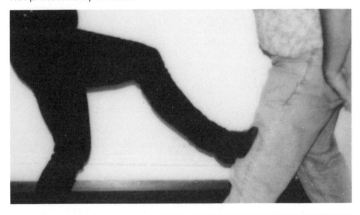

Knee strike   Raise your knee swiftly to the groin; this is used at close range, for example when you are too close to kick.

COUNTER-ATTACKS WITH YOUR ARMS

Palm strike   Place your hand at the centre of your body at about chest height and drive your palm forward; pull your fingers back and use the heel of your palm to hit under the jaw or the nose, or perhaps to the chest if it's a less threatening attack. Practise hitting yourself lightly under the jaw with your palm—it's very powerful, isn't it? Imagine doing it with your full power.

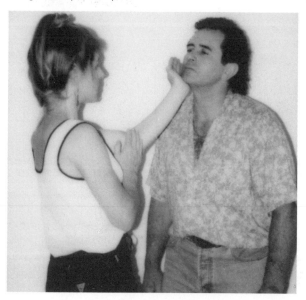

Punch Similar to a palm strike except that the fist is held in a relaxed vertical position and you firm your wrist as the punch approaches its target—the jaw, nose, perhaps the throat if it's a life-threatening attack or to the body if it's a minor attack.

To make a fist, wrap your thumb around the outside of your fingers.

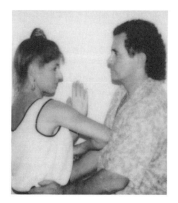 

Elbow strike   Relax your arm with your elbow bent, then swiftly aim the point of your elbow to the jaw, chest or throat.

DEFENCES WITH YOUR ARM

You will be able to neutralise more of the attacker's force if you keep the optimum angle in your arm and if your arm remains moving upon impact.

Upper deflection   Raise your arm from the centre in this fixed angle for any attack coming towards your head or face; raise both arms if the attacker is using both of his.

Lower deflection Move your arm down swiftly at the optimum angle to redirect any attack or grab coming in at midsection height.

ATTACKS FROM THE SIDE

COUNTER-ATTACKS WITH YOUR LEGS

Low side kick Drive the force from the hip and body through your heel as you thrust your leg to the side, aiming to the knee.

Stamp on the instep This can be used against minor attacks or as a way of distracting him with enough pain to enable you to do your next move. Stamp on your own instep to get a feel for the power in this; imagine the effect if you had heeled shoes on.

COUNTER-ATTACKS WITH YOUR ARM

Elbow strike   Swing your bent arm straight out with the point of your elbow aimed to the head area (jaw, face, throat) or to the body (most effective to the solar plexus).

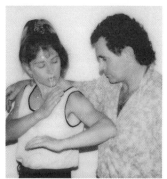

Side slash   Swing your whole arm freely from the shoulder, starting with a bent position similar to the elbow strike position—if he is close you can hit him with the elbow, if he is further away, with your forearm or hand. Allow the forearm to extend as your arm swings out and drive your force through the side of your hand. A strike with the edge of the hand can be powerful, but you may feel more comfortable clenching your fist, especially if striking to a hard target like the jaw. Practise giving yourself a light strike on the side of the jaw with the edge of your hand or fist—this gives you a clue as to how powerful this strike can be.

Punches and palm strikes can also be used to the side.

DEFENCES WITH YOUR ARM

Upper and lower deflections   Raise your arm or cut down with the same structure shown for front defences (see page 51).

ATTACKS FROM BEHIND

COUNTER-ATTACKS WITH YOUR LEGS

Back kick Relax your leg and swing your heel straight back into the shin, knee or groin.

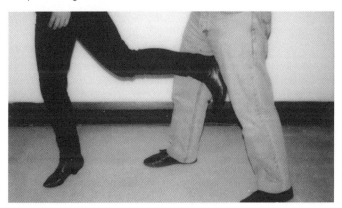

Scrape your heel down his shin.

Stamp on the instep Just as it is when used to counter an attack from the side (page 54), this is a useful preliminary to getting free from a grab—for example, a bearhug from behind—or in a minor situation, it may be enough on its own.

COUNTER-ATTACKS WITH YOUR ARM

Elbow strike   Jab straight back with your elbow to the solar plexus or the head.

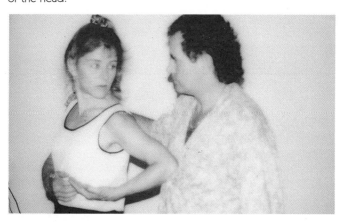

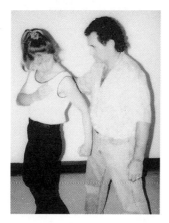

Backfist punch   Swing your fist straight down and back into the groin.

APPLYING YOUR TOOL BOX TO COMMON ATTACKS

Many physical attacks on women start with some kind of grabbing, whether it be to the arm, body, throat or hair. A good way to react to someone grabbing you is to strike them before they can actually grab, as shown on page 59. If you have already been grabbed, it is much easier to get out of the grip if you react immediately. If you are already being grabbed strongly, hit really hard to make the attacker let go. Avoid or minimise struggling and wrestling; save your energy for sharp, sudden, decisive actions. Do try to react quickly because the grab may be a prelude to further attacks.

COUNTER-ATTACKING AN ARM GRAB

As soon as the attacker reaches to grab your arm, react immediately with a palm strike to his chest and move your arm away from his grab. If the attacker has already grabbed your arm, cut down swiftly using the lower deflection, as shown on page 54, and strike with your palm to his jaw. Notice how this also protects against his other hand, which is raised ready to strike.

If the attacker grabs both your arms, cut down with the same swift action and kick him to the knee or shin. The structure of your lower deflection 'attacks' the weakest part of his grip where thumb meets forefinger. By keeping your arm in this shape, relaxing your shoulder and cutting down sharply, you are able to use your whole arm rather than just one set of muscles in the arm.

COUNTER-ATTACKING A THROAT GRAB

The upper deflection from your Tool Box (see page 53) can be used to guard against many types of attack to the head and neck. It is important to keep the structure firm and use a swift movement.

Start with your hands in the centre and raise them straight up.

Try to react before he gets a grip on your throat. As soon as his hands start moving towards your throat, swiftly raise your arms and kick his knee at the same time.

If he is already grabbing your throat, knee him to the groin as you use the same upper deflection.

COUNTER-ATTACKING A BEARHUG FROM BEHIND

See page 86 about being followed, and what to do if someone is behind you.

As you are grabbed from behind, stamp on his instep to distract him and make him loosen his grip while you pivot your body and drive your elbow back into his solar plexus.

COUNTER-ATTACKING A CHOKEHOLD

React as soon as you feel his grab by pivoting your body as you drive your elbow sharply back into the side of his body. By turning into the crook of his arm you can get a little more breathing space than if you turn the other way.

COUNTER-ATTACKING A GRAB TO THE SHOULDER

Your upper deflection is used to remove a grab from the shoulder and combined here with a palm strike to the chest.

 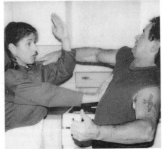

COUNTER-ATTACKING A SLAP TO THE FACE

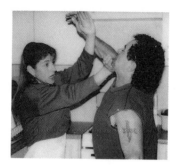

The upper deflection is also an effective way of redirecting a slap or punch to the face, combined here with a punch to the attacker's jaw.

COUNTER-ATTACKING BEING PUSHED OVER

See Using your attacker's force against him on page 41.

As the attacker moves in to push you, steady yourself into a balanced position and let the force of his push turn your whole body; move one arm to the upper deflection position while your other arm strikes him along the centre line with a punch or palm strike.

COUNTER-ATTACKING BEING PULLED

See Using your attacker's force against him on page 41. This technique refers to being pulled into a car, room, building, alley, etc.

As the attacker pulls you, relax into a balanced position and let your whole body go with the force of his pull; depending on which arm he grabs, you can use an elbow strike or a palm strike to his jaw or solar plexus.

COUNTERING AN ATTACK WHEN YOU'RE LYING DOWN

See Bedroom attack on pages 78–80 for a wide range of responses. If you don't have time to get up as the attacker approaches, bend your knees so you can kick easily; use a low heel kick to the groin or midsection.

If he approaches from the side, you can use a side slash to his head, neck or chest.

COUNTERING AN ATTACK WHEN YOU'RE SITTING DOWN

If you don't have time to stand up, you can use a low heel kick to the knee, giving you a chance to stand up and follow on with an elbow strike to the head or, if it's a less serious attack, a palm strike to the chest.

If an attacker sneaks up from the side and tries to silence or strangle you with a scarf, swing your backfist punch straight to his groin.

COUNTER-ATTACKING A PUNCH

Be prepared to react to a punch; this may well be coming if you start to resist and he attacks even harder.

With both hands guarding your centre, notice how quickly you can use one hand to defend and the other to attack; combine your upper deflection with a punch to his jaw.

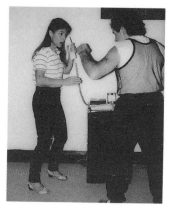 

He may try to use force to stop you from calling for help; as his punch comes towards your face, use a simple palm movement to redirect it while kicking his leg at the same time.

If his punch comes from the side, use your upper side deflection at the same time you kick him with your low side kick.

Develop a clear awareness of your own abilities and the options available. If and when you do fight back use your complete concentration. Think of how you might deal with a poisonous snake or spider that threatens your safety — use decisive movements and be ready to follow up. If the attacker puts up a resistance, continue fighting, make a lot of noise or run away.

How to develop your power

Stance   Place your feet about shoulder-width apart so you have a good base of support with your weight evenly spread over both feet and knees slightly bent, ready to move or kick. Experiment to discover a position that is both stable and mobile for you.

Posture   Stand upright and firm around the waist so you remain balanced when you move or strike; when you bend, part of your body mass moves away from the direction of your strike, thus reducing your power. Bending can also endanger your balance.

Centre line   Face the attacker front-on so you can use your whole body mass and strike quickly to effective targets.

Coordination   Practise moving your body at the same time and in the same direction as your strike—for example, step forward as you punch.

Relaxation   The more relaxed you are, especially in your arms and legs, the quicker your reactions will be; relaxed movements save energy and give less warning to the attacker. Tense movements are slower, use more effort and often telegraph to the attacker. Being physically and mentally relaxed helps you to use your energy most efficiently. Practise relaxing your arm or leg before you do any movement; firm your muscles just before the point of impact.

Concentration   Practise focusing your mental and physical power so that you can eliminate all other thoughts, distractions and doubts; muster all your determination so you can mentally drive your power into the attacker.

Vulnerable targets   Strike to points that will create the most impact (for example, on the centre line), using rapid continuous striking if necessary.

Structural efficiency   Use shapes and parts of your body that are structurally strong—for example the fixed elbow for deflection, the heel of your foot or palm for striking.

Chapter 6

KEY CONCEPTS FOR YOUR SAFETY

We all plan our lives to a certain degree, making decisions about what to do, where to go, when and with whom. This section will help you to make the best decisions for your safety. Many of these simple steps will save you a lot of worry because their emphasis is on prevention. One small point may make the difference for you between being attacked or not, and you will feel more relaxed knowing you have done everything you can. The emphasis is on you being in control rather than on feeling paranoid. Most safety-enhancing decisions cost very little time and effort, and the immediate payoff to you is a feeling of greater freedom and confidence.

THINK AHEAD

Place

• Where are you? Where are you going?
• What potential risks could there be? Are there people around or is the place deserted?
• Are you on familiar or unfamiliar territory?

Think about any places where you feel vulnerable and decide what you can do to maximise your safety.

People

• Who are you with? Who will you be seeing? How well do you know them? What kind of people are they?
• Who knows where you are? Who expects you at a certain time and place?

•What would they do if you didn't turn up?

Consider letting key people know your movements, think about people in your life who can assist you to feel safer, think about any who may pose a potential risk.

Time

•Is it day or night? Is the area dark or well-lit?
•Who is around at this time?

Think about the optimum times for doing different things and plan ahead to minimise risks. Most women report feeling more vulnerable at night in dark, deserted areas. While more attacks happen at night, women are also attacked in broad daylight.

Clothes

•What are you wearing? How appropriate is it for where you are going and any potential risks you may face?
•How much freedom of movement do your clothes allow for running away, for fighting back?
•What about your shoes? Could you run in them? How balanced would you be if you had to defend yourself? Would your shoe(s) be a good weapon—for example, to stamp on the instep or to take off and hit the attacker?
•Will unwanted attention be attracted by the way you are dressed? Are there some situations where you might choose to wear a big dark coat over your party dress?

Think ahead to the situations you will be in, and choose the most appropriate clothing and footwear for your comfort, self-esteem and safety.

Baggage and other items

•What are you carrying? How cumbersome are your bags and parcels?
•Is it necessary to carry them all right now? What if you had to drop them and run?
•What items of value are you carrying? Are you wearing obviously valuable jewellery that someone might try to grab? Are you carrying valuables in your bag that you don't need?

- Is there a baby, small child(ren), an elderly companion with you? This changes your safety options, especially running away.
- What other items do you have that could be useful—for example, a coat or jumper to put over the nearest arm if approached by an attacker with a knife, a briefcase to intercept a knife attack, an umbrella, squash racquet, biro, rolled-up newspaper, belt or other object to fight back with?

Give some thought to what you usually carry; take with you only what you need.

At home

Doors and windows

- Make your home secure—deadlocks on doors, strong security screen doors, peepholes so you can see who is there; keylocks, grilles, secure fastenings on windows.
- Draw blinds and curtains, especially if you are undressing or are alone.
- Choose safe places to put keys.
- Change the locks if you have moved into a new home.

If you are renting, discuss these matters with your landlord or agent. Most landlords appreciate an involved tenant. If you live in an unsafe place and cannot get the landlord's cooperation, do what you can and plan to move as soon as possible.

Outside

- Do not leave ladders or other items around that would help an intruder to gain entry.
- Bring all tools inside or keep them locked away.
- Have outdoor lights installed for when you come in at night, to deter would-be intruders and to turn on when you hear a noise outside.
- Prune overhanging bushes so there is nowhere for an intruder to hide.

Neighbours

- Get to know the people living around you and set up an informal neighbourhood watch system. Let them know your movements if you trust them. Consider pre-arranging a distress signal so you can come to each other's assistance.

- If anything suspicious happens discuss it with your neighbours and let the police know. Sometimes this information can be vital in helping to put a picture together.
- Go to local Neighbourhood Watch meetings, at least occasionally, to get a feel for what is going on in your area. It can be useful to know what the common crimes are, and how and when they are committed. You will gain an overview and perhaps some hints that help you to be safer.

If you live alone

- Be very careful who you tell that you live alone and where you live. Withhold this information from anyone who even indirectly could pose a threat to your safety.
- If you advertise in the paper or on a local noticeboard, be careful about using your name in a way that reveals you are a woman and revealing your phone number. Some women receive obscene phone calls after placing such advertisements. Prepare your ad without a name or put in a male name; when you answer the phone, speak on that imaginary person's behalf.
- Be even more careful about making your address known. In some cases women are attacked by prospective 'buyers' responding to the ad. Casually let any such people know that you are not vulnerable—for example, 'What time are you coming, Mr Smith? I'll put our dog on a chain' or 'If I'm busy, I'll get my husband to show you the fridge'. Have someone with you, or pretend that someone is there or is arriving any minute.
- Consider an unlisted phone number. If your number is listed, simply put your initials rather than a female first name. Attackers sometimes use the telephone directory as a resource. Do the same on the name card at the front of your place—for example, S.V. Brown, not Susan Brown.
- If you are involved in any public exposure, such as that generated by an article in the paper, do not give information that

could be used by an attacker—for example, your surname and the suburb you live in. A woman was assaulted in her home as a result of her name, suburb and photo appearing in the paper. The attacker simply looked her up in the directory.

Date rape

If you are going out with someone new, it may be best to meet somewhere safe—for example, at a restaurant—rather than having him pick you up at home. Until you know him well it is safer that he doesn't know where you live, especially if you live alone. Be aware if you have been drinking, as this can affect your perceptions and judgment. Take a taxi home if you don't have your own car. Be wary about accepting lifts from people and even more careful about inviting them in or going to their place.

Visitors

Keep a careful eye on people who visit the house, like salespeople and tradespeople. Keep details of their visits: their name, company name, date, purpose of visit and any other relevant information. Do not give any information beyond what is absolutely necessary—for example, don't mention that you live alone, that your husband is away, or tell when you are usually home or out. Often when a crime is committed at someone's home police suspicion turns to people who have visited or been in that home recently.

A knock at the door

- Have a look before you open the door, even if you are expecting someone.
- If you can't see the caller call out in a confident tone, 'Who is it?'. If you don't know him, ask who he is, where he is from and what he wants. If the reply sounds suspicious or you do not want to open the door, say you are busy or not interested.
- If you think the caller is genuine but you still do not want to open the door, ask him to leave a card under the door or in the letterbox, or confirm their identity with a phone call while he waits outside.
- If your sixth sense is alerted consider calling the police and

make sure you watch him leave—someone could try to slip around the back. Some attackers and thieves operate door-to-door. Police may have had other reports.

- If you have opened the door but start to feel suspicious, slam the door shut immediately, especially if the caller starts to move in a way that makes you feel unsafe.
- If he blocks the door with his foot or tries to push his way in as you close it, here are some options:
  - shout loudly
  - stamp on his foot
  - kick to his knee
  - push him away
  - punch or palm strike to his face or midsection
  - have an umbrella or broom handy—grab it and use it.

As the attacker blocks the door with his foot and starts to come in, you can . . .

stamp on his foot;

kick his knee;

palm strike to his chest;

punch his face;

have a broom or mop in your hand so that if he forces his way in you can use a straight thrusting action to stop or strike him with it.

Inside the home

- If you do let the person in, stay behind them rather than in front of them. You can keep a close eye on what they are doing, and have all your limbs ready for action; always be wary of turning your back on a potential attacker.
- If you still feel even a fraction uncertain, have that broom, umbrella or rolling pin in your hand.
- When you are at home alone or with children, be careful about situations where you could be taken by surprise—for example, leaving the back door unlocked or windows open if you are busy in another part of the house. Think of the situations in which you could be most vulnerable—for example, in the

Position yourself behind him rather than in a vulnerable position where he could easily attack you.

shower or when the noise of household appliances might cover the sound of an intruder.

- If you are inside a well-secured house and hear a noise outside, *relax*. Think it through logically—you are in a much stronger position than the intruder. If someone tries to break in, here are some suggestions:
  - turn off the indoor lights so he can't see you or your movements
  - turn on all the outside lights so everyone can see him
  - move quietly and listen for where he is; make sure all points of entry are secured
  - grab something you can use as a self-defence weapon—it often makes you feel stronger
  - call the police.
- If the intruder is already on his way in—for example he has broken a window and is climbing in—grab a nearby object like a frying pan, run to where he is entering and hit him. Think of how vulnerable, how unbalanced, how unprepared he is for this. *The powerful surprise element is on your side nearly every time you choose active resistance.*

  He was in the window up to his waist. He said, 'I have a knife. Be quiet!' My hands reached for anything and grabbed the stem

If you catch an attacker already on his way in, grab a heavy object and hit him with it.

of a potted plant in front of the window. I began beating him with the pot . . . I hit him with everything my hands could grab. He finally pulled himself from the window and started to run away. (Groves & Caignon: 1989, p. 131)

- Call out in a loud, strong voice to your attacker—tell him the police are on the way.
- Pretend to be talking to someone—for example: 'John, grab the carving knife and come to the window, I've got the hammer—someone's trying to get in. Boy, will he get a nasty surprise!'
- Get out of the house and go to a safe place—a neighbour you know is at home, the nearest police station. If you have a small child or children, you may have to grab them very quickly to run with you.
- Depending on the age of your child(ren), talk to them in a careful, positive way about safety. Children are remarkably intelligent and have a strong survival instinct. Enlist their involvement; they may be able to pick up a self-defence weapon, run for help, shout loudly or make a phone call.

In bed

'Stop shouting,' he said. I started kicking and kept kicking and suddenly he was off me, off the bed and out the window, walking away. (Groves & Caignon: 1989, p. 66)

Consider installing a phone extension by your bed with

relevant numbers programmed in so you can reach help at the press of a button. If you hear a noise, get up straight away to find out what it is, otherwise you may worry and become frightened. Arm yourself mentally by getting in touch with your survival instincts; arm yourself physically as well by grabbing a nearby object. Usually it is normal house noises like a branch scraping the window, a door creaking in the breeze.

One way of psyching yourself up is to talk aloud as you go to investigate the noise—for example growling, threatening, telling them what you're going to do to them: 'If I catch you I'm going to hit you so hard you'll never do this again.' I know of a woman who stomps through the house as she searches, kicking the doors open, banging a few things. This can make you feel stronger as well as deterring anyone who may be there. Check everywhere that an intruder could gain entry or hide to put your mind at rest. If you do find someone there, you may choose a course of action from the options outlined above.

How you react depends on your ability and confidence. You may get away or you may leave a path open for him to flee; you may trap or lock him in a room. If you are lying in bed and wake to find an intruder in the room, jump up immediately; you are in a much better position for everything, be it running, shouting or fighting, when you are standing up than when you are lying down.

If you are actually attacked while in bed, throw the covers off and strike with all your force (see section on Power, page 69). While it is easier to fight back when you are standing up because you have better balance, can apply your whole body force and can use both your arms and legs, there are still many effective self-defence movements you can use lying down.

Think through the many resources you have:
• Even if the attacker pins your arms down, what about your legs? You may be able to kick or use your knee.
• What about a head butt straight onto his nose as he leans towards your face?
• What about using your elbow, fist or palm to strike?
• Biting is a possibility, especially through clothing which could

 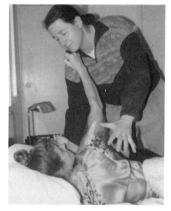

Throw off the covers if you can and kick him to the midsection or groin as he moves in.

If your arms are free, you may use a punch as he attacks.

minimise the risk of communicable diseases.

• What about scratching, pinching, pulling his hair? If you pinch, grabbing a small piece of flesh and twisting will hurt more than a handful.
• What about your voice and all the different ways you can use it?
• Are there any items you can grab like a bedside lamp, table, shoe, book?
• How easily can he hold you down, immobilise your whole body, defend against your fighting responses, remove clothing and assault you?

Your determination to resist makes it a lot harder for an attacker. Do your best to make sure he can't get near your face to try and put something like chloroform over your mouth and nose. If this happens, try to hold your breath or breathe out while you react instantly. Shout loudly, turn the light on, keep fighting or run to safety. Although it may be difficult to hold your breath because often in shock we take a sharp breath in, even holding it for a couple of seconds may allow you enough time to react effectively.

Arriving home

> *Kerry came home from shopping one afternoon and found an intruder removing window louvres. He was about to climb in when he saw her come through the back gate. He looked like a desperate animal about to be caught. Kerry knew her self-defence ability was limited so she swiftly moved out of his way indicating that she was opening a path for him. He ran immediately. She felt enormously relieved.*

If you know your home is very secure, it is unlikely there is an intruder inside. Not having deadlocks or secured windows makes it more likely that you could disturb an intruder. A thief may want to escape but an attacker intent on sexual assault may be hiding in the house waiting.

If there are any signs of intrusion, it may be best not to go in, especially alone. Call the police and wait for them, or go to a neighbour and ask them to come in with you. Unless you are confident of your fighting ability and have a suitable weapon with you, it is probably better not to go in.

Think about the kind of objects they may have used to break in—screwdriver, jemmy, tyre lever; these could be lethal weapons they might try to use on you if you catch them by surprise.

Remember that home is your familiar territory; the other person is the intruder, and they know it. You have lots of advantages over them: you know the layout of the house, the entry and exit points, which objects can be used as weapons and where they are, which internal doors can be locked or barricaded. If you make it too difficult or risky for them, they will probably flee.

AT SOMEONE ELSE'S PLACE

A significant proportion of assaults on women take place in the attacker's home. Make sure someone trusted knows where you are and what time you are expected. Be aware of who else is there. In any potentially vulnerable situation like sleeping, make sure the room is secure. Use the guidelines throughout this book to maximise your awareness of any dangers.

At work

Many women regard work as a safe place, so it can be a shock to realise that women are attacked at work.

- Run a similar checklist to that for your home: be aware of entry and exit points, possible weapons for you and an attacker, familiarise yourself with neighbours, get to know who is usually around at different times, find out how far away help is—the phone, customers, neighbours, workmates.
- Pinpoint specific dangers—for example, do you have to handle money, take money to the bank, open or close up, work back late at night, travel, carry valuable items? Become familiar with the factors that apply at your workplace.
- Be aware if you are alone with any male(s) whom you don't fully trust, especially if working back late or accepting a lift home.

    I had known M for about six months. We were friends and participated in social events with fellow employees. I used to think I could judge people pretty well . . . I was wrong! . . . I was held abducted for twenty long and painful hours, raped nine times, then he released me expecting to go out to dinner with me the following night . . . he'd threatened to kill me, I had a rope around my neck at one stage and I couldn't breathe.
    (Breckenridge & Carmody: 1992, p. 165)

- Be aware of power relations at work, particularly with people who may try to abuse their power. Immediately report any unacceptable behaviour.
- Find a trusted mentor(s) at work and outside of work whom you can confide in and rely on for support.
- If there is someone your instincts warn you about, ensure that you are not alone with him. If you can't avoid this, make your messages to him very clear. Do not turn your back on him; stay in positions where you can see what he is doing.

- Be careful at work social functions where people drink heavily and become overly friendly. Give clear, strong messages. Stay with people you can trust.
- Be aware of potential risks involved in extra-curricular work duties like travelling with your boss, going to work on the weekend, dropping work at a co-worker's place or vice versa.
- If you go to work early, watch to see who is around. If in doubt—for example, if a suspicious looking person is hanging about—don't go into a deserted workplace, go to where people are.
- If you work back late, arrange for someone you trust to be with you, to leave the building with you and escort you to your transport. If this isn't possible ask someone to meet you; at least let someone trusted know your times and movements. Ensure you have a safe way of getting home.
- If opening or locking up the premises, have your keys ready and look around thoroughly; don't leave your back unguarded—turn side-on, change position, watch for movements, shadows and reflections, so that you have warning if anyone approaches.

Handling money
- If your job involves handling money, check on complete details of the company's insurance policy; make sure you know the exact guidelines and procedures.
- If you are accosted by a thief, don't risk your safety. Money can be replaced—you can't.
- Arrange to have someone with you when handling large sums of money, and do not count or handle money where people can see you.
- If you lock up at night, arrange for the till to be cleared earlier—for example, by your boss or co-worker.
- If you carry money to the bank, arrange for someone to go with you, perhaps a couple of steps behind so they can watch closely for any dangers to you. Change your routine so you don't cover the same path at the same time.
- Don't talk about how much money is handled at work; it can

plant ideas in people's minds, and you never know who might be listening.

Dealing with clients

People who work in areas with extensive public contact may face certain risks, including robbery of money and goods, and aggressive or threatening behaviour. These situations include:

- *Welfare work*   Social work, youth work, field work, counselling, working in the office/reception area of a welfare agency, private or government. Working with a wide range of clients, some of whom are experiencing personal and financial problems, can bring an increased risk of violence.

- *Health work*   Community nursing, working in a hospital, a psychiatric hospital, as an ambulance officer, in a doctor's or dentist's surgery. These areas may pose the risk of both aggressive behaviour and robbery of money and possibly drugs.

- *Security and police work*   The risks are more obvious here as the actual work role involves protection of people and property.

- *Retail, banking*   Both outlets may be a target for robbery. Certain types of business have a higher risk profile than others—for example, jewellery stores and pharmacies. Any business that handles items of value and money could be a target.

- *Service occupations*   All forms of consultation, including services that are brought into the home—for example, personal fitness consultant, masseur, delivery person.

Many workplaces have procedures designed to minimise risks and maximise safety. Go through these with your workmates, management and union or association. Thoroughly examine the guidelines, assess their usefulness, and then modify, add and adapt them to your own particular work role. Clarify and resolve any outstanding concerns you have. If you are new to the job, speak to the people you work with about their experiences and any advice they may have. If you feel the risks are high, consider organising a specialised self-defence course at work (make sure you find a qualified instructor). Many employers support these initiatives because they enhance safety and morale, and can reduce the injury, stress and illness resulting from violence.

If you work alone, look closely at the various security and alarm systems available. It may be worth investing in an easy-to-use system, that is well positioned and has a 'back to base' response system.

When you assess the risks of your particular work situation, look to see how the advice in this book could be adapted to your circumstances. Make a risk analysis of the various things that have occurred and are likely to occur in your work environment. Compare notes with people in similar organisations; they may have some sound advice based on their own experiences.

On the street

- Look and feel confident—you have the right to be there and to be safe as you go about your life.
- In an unfamiliar area, deliberately adopt the body language of inner power so you don't look lost and vulnerable.
- Walk well away from alleys, doorways, alcoves where someone could hide.
- Look into doorways and lanes as you pass to ensure there isn't someone there who could slip out and attack from behind once you've passed.
- Feel free to look around as much as you like; if you pass someone suspicious, look around as if taking in the whole view; show that you are in control of your territory.
- Be prepared for what you are doing and where you are going with anything you need ready at hand so you don't have to search in your bag.
- In quiet, dark streets, some people walk down the middle of the road where it is well lit and you can see if anyone is approaching; you are also away from shrubbery and fences where an attacker could hide.
- Be aware of your body positioning and don't turn your back on potential danger.

If your attention is occupied, choose the safest position where you can't be taken by surprise.

For example:

- When reading a map for directions, move to where you can keep your back against a wall.
- When using an ATM, stand side-on, look around and move a little, watch for movement and reflection.
- When making a call in a phone box, stand facing outwards rather than with your back to an open door; look around so you are aware of anyone approaching.
- If you're standing in a queue and someone unpleasant is pressing into you from behind, hold your arms slightly out from your body at their optimum angle and turn around; create a larger space around you, move in it, don't allow them into it.
- Walking down the street, use your arms at their optimum angle to create more space around you and redirect anyone who may jostle or bump you.

Are you being followed?

Be aware at all times of anyone behind you. Even if you don't hear footsteps, look around frequently and confidently as if you have every right to know what is going on. Once I was followed by a man in soft-soled shoes that made no sound. I only saw him because my sixth sense told me to look behind. It is important to establish quickly who is behind you, how close they are and if you feel they may pose a threat to your safety.

If there is someone behind you, how can you tell whether they are following you? Take a look to see who it is; even a quick glance gives you lots of information. If you feel too obvious doing this, you can:

- Look in shop windows as you pass, focusing on the reflection behind.
- Turn sideways to cross the road and have a thorough look while you seem to be checking for cars.
- Turn around and go back towards the person, as if you have a purpose for completely changing direction; if you want an

A quick glance behind enables you to assess the situation.

Cross the road, having a good look behind.

apparent reason, look at your watch or pretend you've forgotten something.

If what you see and feel concerns you, don't ignore the warning. If you're not concerned, simply go on your way. If he follows you across the road you can:

•Turn back in the direction you've come from; if he still follows, be ready for flight or fight.
•Run away.
•Go into a shop.
•If there are safe-looking people nearby, go up and talk to them as if you know them.

If he follows you across the road, running away is a possibility; see pages 24–6 for further details.

If there is someone nearby like a neighbour, go up and talk to them to deter the person following you.

I knew I had to do something fast. I knew I couldn't run away fast enough. Then I got an idea. Another man was coming up on the other side of the street . . . so I pretended that he was my dad. I said, 'Hey Dad. Hey, Dad, wait, hey Dad!' And the attacker started getting really shaky, and the other man turned around and I just kept saying, 'Hey Dad, I forgot I have to tell you something, I'd like you to meet my friend.' So the attacker let go his grip on my shoulder, and I was walking real fast across the street . . . this man is looking at me really puzzled . . . next thing I know, the attacker split. (Groves & Caignon: 1989, p. 18)

Turn and face them confidently:

- Speak firmly, perhaps ask a question so they have to respond to you. Sometimes they are thrown off if you take verbal control of the situation (see pages 26–32).
- Confront them directly: 'What are you doing?'
- Threaten them: 'Get away from me! I'll give you three seconds . . . one . . . two (see page 31).
- Step forward with your guard up, ready for action.

If the person is right behind you and about to attack, *turn around immediately* and face them front-on. You have a lot more resources from this position. You can use either arm, both arms at the same time, and either leg, quickly and easily, both for

Turn around with your guard up as he tries to grab you.

From here you are ready to act.

You can parry his arms out of the way and hit him, or if he tries to punch, you can use your upper deflection combined with a punch and a kick.

attack and defence, with the full power of your body behind your movement. (See Power and Centre line on page 44 for more detail.) If you don't have time to turn around, you can use the side slash or stamp and elbow strike from your Tool Box.

As he grabs you from behind, stamp to his instep so he loosens his grip while you pivot and elbow strike into his midsection.

Handbag theft

Be aware of what you are carrying; as you look around for signs of potential threat, simple changes in how you carry your bag(s) can keep your valuables safer and leave one arm free for action.

•Keep a tight grip on your handbag so it can't be grabbed easily by someone swooping past from behind.

•Listen carefully for any sounds of someone coming from behind.

•Look around thoroughly for any warning signs.

If you see a suspicious-looking person or group up ahead, put all your bags on the side furthest away from them; walk past with as much distance as possible between you and them so you have more time to react if they go for you or your bag. Keep your bag out of their reach and have the arm close to them ready for defence and counter-attack. If they do move towards you, you are ready.

If you see someone suspicious up ahead and you have bags in both arms, move them to the side further away from him.

If he reaches for your bag, use the lower deflection combined with a palm strike to his face.

If you can sling the bag on your shoulder, both arms are free for self defence. Some women feel more comfortable carrying their bag across the body, but others feel they could be pulled over and hurt if a determined thief were after their bag. This also depends on whether you are aware of the attacker's approach and how strongly you can resist.

Should you hand over your bag?

It depends on the specific situation, and only you can answer this. How confident are you about using a wide range of

As the thief comes from behind to grab your bag, turn towards him and hit him; use your other hand at its optimum angle to stop him from getting hold of the bag; go with his momentum if he is moving quickly.

If he approaches you front-on and grabs for your bag, use a low heel kick to stop him.

options, including running away, verbal responses, fighting back? Make sure your bag does not contain unnecessary valuables which might lead you to endanger your safety by trying to hold onto them. If you feel the danger is very high you can hand the bag over. Remember that the things in your bag are generally replaceable. Sometimes police advise women to keep their keys and some money in a pocket in case their bag is grabbed.

Keep a spare set of keys well hidden away in case your bag is stolen. Keep a list of the relevant phone numbers handy so you can report the theft immediately, cancel credit cards, etc. (include your credit card numbers on the list).

The motive for handbag theft may be assault as well as theft; handing the bag over could lead to further demands. Be aware too of what is in your bag—keys, name, address, licence—that the thief could use to commit further crimes. The more you can avoid danger and the more safety strategies you can use, the greater chance you have of keeping your bag.

Approaches on the street

Sometimes people come up on the street asking for directions or money. Be careful they are not setting you up for attack or theft. Use all your forward awareness skills so that you are ready. How you react when approached is a personal choice.

These general points are useful in most situations:

- Move your valuables/bag to the other side from where they approach.
- Watch them closely, picking up messages about their intentions.
- Stand back so they don't come into your personal space; this gives you more time and space to react if something happens.
- If they move too close, step away and use your arm positions to protect your space.
- Have a quick look around—are their companions lurking nearby?
- Face them squarely, stand and speak confidently.
- If you can help them, for example, by giving directions, do so promptly and firmly; if not, say so and continue on your way,

The wrong way and the right way: if you need to get something from your bag, step back with your arm up and use your sense of touch to locate what you want.

always keeping an eye on their movements (are they following you?).

- Be very careful if their request involves your attention moving away from them, like getting something from your bag. Keep your bag as far away from them as possible, perhaps stepping back and using your arm to create more space between you.
- Use your hand and sense of touch to find what you want in your bag rather than looking down and thus away from the person.
- If you want to divert their attention while you find something, ask them a question or two, get them talking, put the focus onto them or use some other subtle distraction.
- Establish that you are in control of the situation through your general posture, tone and topics of speech.
- If you feel nervous, move away immediately, keeping an eye on them.

Groups and gangs

If you see a group of people up ahead that makes you feel uneasy, one of the best strategies is quiet avoidance: cross the road or turn into another street well before you come to them. If this isn't possible and you are already in their midst, keep your head

Quiet avoidance is one of the safest strategies; cross the road unobtrusively to avoid walking through a group of suspicious people.

high, put a firm expression on your face and claim your territory. Walk purposefully and choose the safest path past them; calmly expect them to keep out of your way.

It is generally preferable to maintain eye-contact. In a group situation you may choose an eye position that enables you to take in the whole scene; your eyes may move to cover all the

Move confidently as you approach the group; move your arms freely so the arm closer to the group can form a barrier between you and them; walk purposefully.

people in the group. There is often an obvious 'leader' or 'front man'—perhaps the one who will jostle you, stand in your way, make a remark. This could be the main person to make eye-contact with. Some women report that a stern glare can deter an unwanted approach. Such a look can say, 'I'm not interested. I'm strong. Go away. Don't bother me.'

As you walk past the group, make sure your bag is in the safest position, use your arms to create space around you and look as if you have an important destination.

If these deterrents don't work and you are attacked, one of the safest choices is to run away. If you are unable to get away, react immediately with speed, power and determination. The instant any attacker makes a move, counter-attack so quickly

As the first one lunges towards you, use a low heel kick followed by a punch to his face; as the second one strikes, use your upper deflection combined with a palm strike to his jaw; turn immediately and side slash the third attacker as he moves in.

that you take them by surprise. This may give you time to run.

If you can stop the first approach, sometimes you deflate the whole group's intention. In terms of numbers and probability, it is much harder to take on a group than a single attacker, and the danger to you could be greater if you don't get away. However, the more courage you show, the more clear it becomes that you are not the victim they hoped for.

The three guys were coming at us in a row. I decided to go for the nearest one, and I knew I had to be really fast, to catch them off guard . . . I picked up my leg and kicked as hard as I could

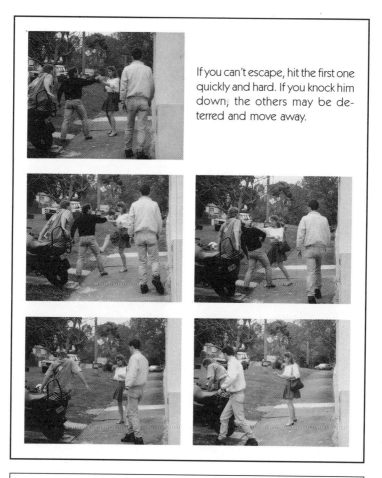

If you can't escape, hit the first one quickly and hard. If you knock him down, the others may be deterred and move away.

Deal with each attacker quickly and decisively; run or call for help as soon as possible.

toward the first guy's groin. He doubled over with this look of shock on his face. The other guy was getting closer, and I slammed the heel of my hand up against the bottom part of his nose . . . and he stopped coming toward me . . . By this time some other men had come and gotten the third guy and held him . . . For me that was one of the most empowering experiences I've had, knowing that I could defend myself by just being real fast and accurate and not thinking that I would get hurt more if I hurt these guys. (Groves & Caignon: 1989, p. 154)

When fighting a group:

- Have every possible strategy ready—for example, run the moment you can safely get away; use your verbal skills, perhaps shouting loudly, creating a scene, especially if there are other people around.
- Display total confidence in your ability and show your determination to resist.
- Move strategically—don't walk into the middle where they can all attack you at once.

- Try to keep your back to a wall or an area where they can't get behind you.
- Position yourself so that only one person can reach you at a time—this may involve shifting position as you lash out at each attacker; this positioning gives you valuable split seconds to be ready for the next attack.
- Respond instantly to an attack with all your power so that you create the most effect possible.
- If you hit the first attacker hard, the others may think twice before attacking you.

USING TRANSPORT

Know what transport is available and make back-up plans so you are not stranded.

Waiting for the bus, train, ferry

- Check timetables beforehand so you aren't waiting unnecessarily.
- Carry change and a phone card for calls.
- Sit or stand where you have a clear view of everything.
- Keep your back to the wall so no-one can sneak up behind you; be very careful of this when sitting down. Change position if you feel uncomfortable.
- Move around in your space to claim this territory as yours and to keep an eye on everything.

On the bus, train, ferry

- Stay near other people who look helpful and friendly.
- Choose your position carefully: at the back so no-one is behind you, near the driver or guard's carriage, near the aisle so you can get up quickly and are not trapped in your seat.
- If there is a person or group acting suspiciously, move away quietly and confidently, watching them all the time.
- If it is crowded and someone presses against you from behind, use your elbows to create a little space. Even a soft elbow to the midsection, especially the solar plexus, carries a strong message. If the approach is sneaky, your response can be subtle as if you don't actually mean to hit them—for example,

step on his foot. If the approach is overt, you may use a verbal response as well: 'Get your hands off me right now!' Be ready to follow through.

- If you are approached in a threatening way while sitting down, stand up immediately. This usually stops the person from advancing and may prompt him to step backwards, especially if you stand up swiftly and move forward at the same time. Have your arms up ready for action. Combine this action with a verbal response if you wish.
- Standing up gives you more physical and psychological power. Refer back to page 66 for suggestions about what to do if you are attacked while sitting down.
- Many seats are fixed, but if the seat is unsteady you may have to brace yourself as you react.
- If you are attacked, use simple responses from your Tool Box.

Getting off the bus, train, ferry
- Be aware of anyone who may follow you. If you feel unsure, get back on and speak to the driver or another person; otherwise, stay in a public, well-lit area or go into a cafe or shop to shake the person off before continuing on your way.
- If you feel concerned, go to a phone and call a taxi or someone who can come and meet you.
- Avoid deserted, poorly-lit areas. If you have to walk through such areas, stay close to safe-looking people. If you are anxious, start talking to these people, ask if you can come with them or if they can stay while you call a taxi.
- Strike up conversations and acquaintances with other regular travellers; arrange to accompany each other.
- Look around to check that you're not being followed.

Going to your car
- Look around, especially if walking into a deserted carpark; watch for shadows behind pillars, listen for any noises; get away immediately if anything arouses your suspicion.
- Be ready to open the door and get straight in.
- If your car is unlocked or could have been tampered with, quickly check that no-one is hiding in it. In one situation, a woman was assaulted by someone hiding in the back who

attacked when she started driving.

Driving

- Keep the doors locked while driving through unsafe areas.
- Keep an eye on your rear and side mirrors to see who and what is around you.
- If someone comes up to your car, don't wind the window down if you feel unsafe; they can speak to you through the window. If you do wind the window down, take it down only a few centimetres so they can't attack you.
- Use the horn to attract attention and to scare them away.
- Remember that you are reasonably safe in your car; it is not easy for someone to get in if the doors are locked; you can drive somewhere safe, like home, a police station, a petrol station or a busy area with lots of people around.

Precautions

- Keep your car well-maintained, especially if going on a long trip. Keep the petrol tank filled up so there is little chance of running out at an inconvenient time and place.
- Keep some safety items in your car in case it breaks down: perhaps a torch, whistle, pen and paper, walking shoes, jacket, umbrella.
- Let someone know your movements so they'll be alerted if you don't arrive on time.

If your car breaks down

What you do depends on where you are, what potential risks there are to your safety, what help is available, and whether you can get the car going yourself.

> One night I was driving home late, and my car broke down on an isolated freeway section. Instead of staying with my car, I decided to move into a position where I had a choice about who would help me. I got my umbrella, changed into running shoes and walked very purposefully until I reached a set of traffic lights. I quickly but deliberately glanced in the four or five cars at the lights, and chose the people I felt safest approaching for help—two women. (personal interview)

- If there is a phone nearby walk to it quickly and confidently.
- Be aware and assertive with anyone who stops to help you.
- Carry an umbrella or something from your car's tool kit if it makes you feel safer.

Getting out of your car

- Look in your rear and side view mirrors before you get out.
- Have your keys ready as you arrive home so you can go in quickly.
- Watch as you walk so that no-one falls in behind you or steps out from bushes.
- If in doubt, stay in the car and drive somewhere safer.

In a taxi

A number of young women experience harassment from taxi drivers. You can minimise the risk by following these suggestions:

- Sit in the back.
- Have a good look at the driver's ID which is usually on the dashboard and can be seen clearly when sitting in the back.
- Pay attention to his manner and actions, including where he is taking you.
- If he makes suggestive remarks or seems to be going in the wrong direction, order him to drive to your destination immediately. Use a firm tone to show you are in control. If he doesn't respond, you could say: 'I'm going to report you; I have your number' or 'Stop here right now. I'm getting out'.
- If he continues to harass you wind down the window and call out to attract the attention of passers-by; get out of the car at the first possible opportunity—for example, at a traffic light.
- Look through your Tool Box to envisage the self-defence responses you could use in a car.

LEISURE AND SOCIAL SITUATIONS

In a park

- Familiarise yourself with your local area and the types of crimes that happen here; avoid areas you believe may be dangerous.

- Move away from any suspicious looking people or groups.
- Carry an umbrella or other useful item that you could use in defence.
- Be careful when using public toilets because a number of attacks happen in them. They are often isolated and women using them are in a vulnerable position. Don't use them if anyone suspicious is nearby. Look around before you go in, thoroughly check each cubicle inside, be careful leaning over the basin with your back turned as you wash your hands, and look around as you're coming out.

At a party

You can usually tell if there are troublemakers at a party from their words and actions, even at an early stage before any real trouble develops. If you get the feeling that things could turn nasty, it may be best to leave now and go somewhere else where you can relax and enjoy yourself. If you don't want to leave, move as far away as possible from the troublemaking group and keep a close eye on their activities. This makes it less likely you will be taken by surprise if one of them falls on you, if drinks are spilt, if glasses or furniture are thrown or broken, or if a fight breaks out. Be very careful if you are near such groups and individuals because their boisterous behaviour can become worse and damage innocent bystanders.

Harassment

If someone harasses you at a party, your body language and verbal skills may be sufficient to deter them. Firm words and actions work best: 'Leave me alone; I'm not interested in you', or 'Go away; I'm here with my husband and friends'.

If he physically intrudes on your space or touches you:
- 'Accidentally' stand on his instep—particularly effective if you're wearing stilettos.
- Fling your arms about in big gestures while talking as if it's part of the story or joke you are telling, 'accidentally' hitting him as a subtle warning for crowding your space; rather than pretending to apologise, say something like 'you'd better move back; you might get hurt'.
- Use your arm positions to keep plenty of space around you

and move your body and arms continuously to keep the person away.

- Pretend to trip slightly, perhaps stepping on his foot at the same time, and spill your drink over him, saying 'You're too close—you've knocked my drink! You'd better clean up.'
- If he puts his hand on your body, move away, stamp or tread on his foot or use the optimum angle arm defence position to remove his hand with a swift action. Glare at him sternly, warn him to stop this behaviour.

If the harassment continues and you don't want to leave, ask other guests or the host for assistance:

- A group of you can use the methods described above; if several people tread on his feet, elbow him and spill drinks on him, he may get the message and move away.
- A group of you can ask him to leave.
- A group of you can 'escort' him to the door and politely make him leave.
- If there is any hint of serious trouble, call the police immediately.

If he actually attacks you, but the attack is more of a nuisance than a real threat to your safety, here are some gentle self-defence ideas:

- Warn him to leave you alone.
- Place your palm on his chest and push him away (see photo on page 76, Coming in doors).
- Use both palms on his shoulders to push him back.
- Use your palm to his jaw or nose with enough power to make him realise you are serious.
- If he is behind or at your side use your elbow.
- If he puts his arms around your waist from front-on, try a knee to the groin, an elbow to the chest or jaw, a palm to the jaw.
- Use any of the fighting techniques shown in this book, regulating the amount of speed and power; do it lightly if you just want to warn him.

Be ready for follow-up action in case he continues to attack you.

At a nightclub or restaurant

Avoid places where you know fighting occurs and follow similar guidelines to those outlined for a party.

With your partner

Being with a man can in some situations be seen by an attacker as provocation rather than protection. Men sometimes pick a fight with another man who is with a woman. If you are out with a male companion and a person or group is paying unwanted attention to you, move away quietly and immediately. Things may worsen as the night goes on and more alcohol is consumed. Behave in a firm, assertive manner, take responsibility for yourself and your actions. This will help prevent the chance that men use you as an excuse for violence.

If you have the type of partner who gets very possessive about you, clarify this whole issue with him at a sensible time and place when you are both sober. Discuss the situation in a calm, assertive way, using 'I' statements rather than 'you' statements; make sure you both express your views, and listen to and understand each other's feelings. Reach a working agreement on how you will behave individually and together while out. Discuss how you would handle an attack and the strategies you can use to complement each other and enhance safety for both of you.

Some people attack couples with the intention of raping the woman. Be aware of this possibility when out with your partner, especially in secluded places.

GOING TO SOMEONE'S ASSISTANCE

This woman single-handedly fought off two attackers, who ran away:

> I was on a street corner, and nobody was getting out of their cars to say, 'Hey, leave that lady alone.' So I thought, well, fight like hell . . . I asked myself, 'Where are all the concerned citizens in this neighbourhood? They're all just kind of driving by and watching to see what happened.' (Groves & Caignon: 1989, p. 178)

We hear many reports of how passers-by ignore the plight of people who need help. People are scared they may get hurt by getting involved. As in all situations that involve your safety, it is up to you to determine your own actions when it comes to helping others in danger. What if it was you? Would you want someone to help? What are the choices? To stand by and see someone innocent get hurt? To pretend it's not happening? Think about what you could do to help others. If you don't want to get physically or verbally involved, you may be able to get help from other people, or to call the police. You may be able to ask the woman in danger if she would like your help, and if so, what? You may be able to provide a distraction like shouting and pointing in another direction to divert the attacker's attention and allow his intended victim some time to get away.

In some situations you may choose to intervene verbally and with your fighting skills: Alison was out at a pub with a girlfriend, listening to a rock band, one Saturday night. She noticed a couple arguing—nearly everyone in the hotel noticed them, so obvious was their conflict. The woman got up and walked out; the man followed almost immediately.

'Oh oh!' said Alison to her friend, 'that doesn't look too good.'

'Don't get involved,' replied her friend, 'let them sort it out.'

'But it looks like he's going to bash her up!' protested Alison. 'What if it was you or me? Would you want everyone to ignore it? Come on! At least we can be there if she wants our help'. They followed the couple out. 'Let me handle it; I'll ask her if she's OK.'

Just at that moment, a police car cruised slowly past. 'Phew!' breathed Alison, stopping. 'Did someone call them or is it just a lucky coincidence?'

Michael was at the bus stop one night; he had just finished his Wing Chun class. An old man was being harassed by three young thugs. They pushed him about and demanded money. He fell to the ground and they started kicking his head. Michael intervened.

'Leave him alone!' he said strongly. One of them turned to him, snarling, 'It's none of your business', as he stepped forward to hit Michael. Michael deflected the blow, kicked him in the groin and punched him to the face. He doubled over, and Michael stepped back to see how the other two would react. One was already moving away, while the other was helping the injured thug to his feet. They quickly disappeared.

Take stock of your resources and strategies in the same way you do for your own safety so that you can decide what help you could offer someone else.

Summary

This book is a contribution to help women on a personal level to say no to violence and to say yes to safety. Every woman can say 'I am of value, I am worth protecting, I have a right to be safe'.

There is a very real need for accurate information about the nature and extent of violence. Violence towards women is still a very large and hidden problem. Compounding this attitude are deep-seated attitudes from thousands of years ago that regard women and children as the property of men. These attitudes remain reflected in our legal and judicial system, and hard as it may be to believe, are the subconscious basis for many of the myths about sexual assault and violence to women that people still believe to this day. But while broader social changes are slowly occurring, women are still being assaulted and raped every day.

The strategies presented here can help you to avoid becoming a victim. I encourage you to claim your body and personal space as your own, and to fiercely protect them in every way you can. This can contribute to a change of attitudes in a wider sense; it sets a positive example to other women and it sends a message of warning to men who use violence.

How can we move beyond the personal sphere to create

solutions to violence? It is tempting to take a simplistic view, and look for superficial causes and answers, but this will not bring about real change. The National Committee on Violence has identified two major factors that relate to the risks of violence:

1 Patterns of relating within families, and their impact on child development: 'Families constitute the training ground for aggression. It is within the family that aggressive behaviours are first learnt.' (From an address by Professor Duncan Chappell, Director Australian Institute of Criminology, to the 1993 Censorship Conference, Sydney, October 1993.)

This is an area in which we all share responsibility for the way we relate within our own families. Is it OK to use physical force within the family, especially to children, or does this give the message that violence is acceptable, particularly towards those who are small, vulnerable and can't fight back?

2 Social attitudes: '. . . The use of violence to achieve ends perceived as legitimate is a principle deeply embedded in Australian culture. Violence on the sporting field, in the home and in schools is tolerated by many Australians.' (ibid)

Social attitudes often reflect values learnt at home. As long as significant proportions of the community consider violence normal and acceptable there is no reason for it to diminish.

Inequalities between men and women also need to be addressed to achieve a reduction in violence. As the status of women has risen, we are seeing two major crimes—sexual assault and domestic violence—gradually coming into the open, providing a basis for changes in attitudes and behaviour. As long as these problems remain hidden, their true dimensions are unknown and there is little that can be done to change them.

As well as funding and expanding the agencies that help victims and apprehend offenders, we need to focus on improving relations between women and men.

Men and women need to join together against violence and sexual assault, to ensure that these crimes are prevented, resisted, reported, investigated and prosecuted. We need to work on reshaping the personal, social and legal values that allow these crimes to flourish and damage a huge proportion among us. This can be a step towards redefining our attitudes towards power—to discard the notion of power as domination or aggression, and to replace it with concepts of integrity, equality and mutual respect.

BIBLIOGRAPHY

Books

Jan Breckenridge & Moira Carmody (eds) (1992) *Crimes of Violence—Australian responses to rape and child sexual assault*, Allen & Unwin, Sydney
Particularly useful for those who work in the area of sexual assault.

Jessica Davies (1990) *Protect Yourself—A Woman's Handbook*, Judy Piatkus (Publishers) Ltd, London
One of the better books on women's safety.

Gail Groves & Denise Caignon (eds) (1989) *Her Wits About Her—Self-Defence Success Stories by Women*, Women's Press, London; first published by Harper & Row Inc., New York, 1987
This is an excellent book full of positive stories and helpful information about how women have prevented and resisted attacks.

Nancy Henley (1977) *Body Politics—Power, sex and nonverbal communication*, Prentice-Hall, New Jersey.
A very interesting read on the power relations of body language.

Diana Lamplugh (1991) *Without Fear*, Weidenfeld and Nicolson, London
Contains useful information, especially on communication skills.

John Walker (assisted by Dianne Dagger) (1993) *Crime in Australia*, Australian Institute of Criminology, Canberra
An interesting look at the bigger picture of crime in Australia.

Reports and Bulletins

NSW Health Department (1993) *Victims of Sexual Assault—Initial Contact at NSW Department of Health Sexual Assault Services 1989, 1990, 1991*, prepared by The Women's Health Unit

and The Information Centre, Sydney
Reliable, comprehensive data.

NSW Sexual Assault Committee (1993) *Sexual Assault Phone in Report*, Report of a phone-in held November 1992, NSW Department of Health, Ministry for the Status and Advancement of Women, Sydney
Contains many direct quotes and experiences.

NSW Women's Co-ordination Unit (1992) *NSW Sexual Assault Committee Report*, NSW Women's Co-ordination Unit, Sydney

Pia Salmelainen & Christine Coumarelos (1993) 'Adult Sexual Assault in NSW' in *Crime and Justice Bulletin*, NSW Bureau of Crime Statistics and Research, No. 20: July 1993

Elizabeth Matka (1991) 'Domestic Violence in NSW' in *Crime and Justice Bulletin*, NSW Bureau of Crime Statistics and Research, No. 12: March 1991

—— 'Uses and Abuses of Crime Statistics' in *Crime and Justice Bulletin*, NSW Bureau of Crime Statistics and Research, No. 11: Nov. 1990
These three bulletins present concise, relevant information.

Further reading

Susan Brownmiller (1975) *Against Our Will—Men, Women and Rape*, Simon & Schuster, New York
A landmark book on the subject.

Marcia Walker & Stanley Brodsky (eds) (1976) *Sexual Assault,* Lexington Books

Paul Wilson *(1978) The Other Side of Rape*, University of Queensland Press, Brisbane

Carol V. Horos (1974) *Rape*, Tobey Publishing Co., Connecticut

Lorenne Clark & Debra Lewis (1977) *Rape: The Price of Coercive Sexuality*, Canada

Andra Medea & Kathleen Thompson (1974) *Against Rape*, Farrar Strauss & Giraux, New York

Rape, Prostitution, Pornography, Proceedings of a seminar on the exploitation of persons, 23–24 June 1978, Department of Continuing Education, University of Adelaide

INDEX